£14·95

D1436896

PICASSO
in Catalonia

JOSEP PALAU I FABRE

PICASSO
in Catalonia

CHARTWELL
BOOKS, INC.

Translated by KENNETH LYONS

Reproduction rights SPADEM-Paris

Published by
CHARTWELL BOOKS, INC.
A Division of **BOOK SALES, INC.**
110 Enterprise Avenue
Secaucus, New Jersey 07094

Spanish-language edition:
© *1975 Ediciones Polígrafa, S. A. - Barcelona (Spain)*

ISBN 0 89009 449 7

Library of Congress Catalog Card Number: 81-66871

Dep. Legal: B. 15.246 - 1981
Printed in Spain by La Poligrafa, S. A. - Parets del Vallès (Barcelona)

Summary

To Madame Jacqueline Picasso,
homage from a Catalan in the name of Catalonia

NOTE TO THE SECOND EDITION

The years that elapsed between the great homage rendered to Picasso on the occasion of his eighty-fiftieth birthday in 1966 and the date of his death, 8th April 1973, were of the greatest importance to the greater knowledge and divulgation of his work. This book, indeed, the first edition of which coincided with the former event, was among the first of many such publications and was intended to fill an evident gap.

Today, eight years after its publication, I consider that the general plan and structure of the book are still valid; but the nagging urge to improve and enrich, together with an increasing appreciation of the scientific approach, have induced me to revise the original material and enlarge it to include such additions and elucidations as seemed to be worth making — plus, I might as well admit, corrections wherever these were found necessary.

This work of analysis and criticism has gone on in felicitous parallel to the gradual emergence of quantities of excellent works by Picasso, which have come out of their obscurity over the last few years thanks to reproductions and have made it possible for art lovers to form an increasingly deep and extensive knowledge of this unprecedented *œuvre*.

Thus this new edition of *Picasso in Catalonia*, which the publishers have spared no effort to present as attractively as possible, is above all else a feast for the eyes. To see what Picasso saw, in a way as close as possible to the way in which he saw it at every moment, is equivalent to seeing — and helping others to see — what was perceived over the years by surely the most powerful, alert eyes that have ever existed; it amounts, in short, to enriching our own capacity for seeing and looking.

This gaze of Picasso sweeping over our country is one of the most surprising riches that Catalonia possesses — perhaps without realizing it particularly, or at any rate not realizing it sufficiently. As well as our Picasso Museum in Barcelona, that magnificent materialization of so many happy ties and attachments, there is also (to use a terminology by now familiar to everybody) an "Imaginary Museum of Catalonia by Picasso", which is even more astonishing in its splendour than the other — and no less *real*. Picasso saw certain places in Catalonia at some of the culminating moments in his prophetic vision of the world: we need only recall the time he spent at Gósol in 1906, which might stand for the height of his aspiration to the ideal of beauty, or his stay at Cadaqués in 1910, a major milestone on his way towards abstraction. Thanks to Picasso, indeed, Catalonia has been recorded for ever by the marvellous, hallucinatory vision of the twentieth century. This book is intended, here and now, to be an unimpeachable testimony to the whole.

Barcelona, September 1974

PROLOGUE TO THE FIRST EDITION

This book began to take more or less definite shape when, returning to Catalonia after an absence of fifteen years, I visited Horta de Sant Joan in the Spring of 1961, with my friend Perucho. It seemed absolutely essential to visit all the places where Picasso had stayed in our country, and I even found it surprising that nobody had thought of doing so before.

From this beginning the work went ont gradually; I took advantage of every opportunity to question the friends Picasso still had, from his youth in Barcelona, as well as to visit — or to discover, for I also had this pleasure — the places where he had worked.

In the course of editing the book, a series of difficulties arose, which were partly solved by Picasso himself during a visit (May 8th 1965). But when it came to the definitive editing of the text, I found myself confronted with a second series of difficulties, much greater ones this time and which could only be settled by Picasso personally — for I had exhausted the possibilities of research and consultations. And so this book would have been published with glaring omissions if the painter had not agreed to settle these points in the course of a laborious interview

(September 1st 1965), at the end of which Picasso himself exclaimed: "We've certainly worked hard, haven't we?"

Moreover, when the book was already in progress, I had another friendly interview with him (May 27th 1966), which permitted me to clear up some minor details.

Grifeu (Llançà), October 25th 1966,
eighty-fifth birthday of Picasso.

PART ONE

BARCELONA, 1895-1904

1. Antecedents. The timid renaissance initiated in Catalonia in the very nadir of her decadence, thanks to the tenacity of the Catalans, seems to have gathered a decided impetus with the creation, in Barcelona, of the active Chamber of Commerce (1758), which was to found the School of Fine Arts or "Lonja", and with the decrees of Carlos III permitting the Catalans to trade with America (1778). This process is thought to have reached its highest point with the Universal Exhibition in 1888.

By 1895 Barcelona had leaped over its own walls and had a population of half a million inhabitants. A new life, which seems to have made her forget her immediate past, was beginning for the city. The Barcelona which that adolescent who was now Picasso was to know and contend with, was an adolescent like himself, with all the qualities and defects that that implies: impetuosity, generosity, confusion, excessive initiative, sudden changes of humour, contradictions...

2. The appointment. By Royal Order of March 17th 1895, Don José Ruiz Blasco, official professor of drawing in the School of Fine Arts of Corunna, was authorized to make an exchange of posts with Román Navarro García, professor of the School of Fine Arts of Barcelona, the former being assigned an annual salary of three thousand pesetas. Don José Ruiz Blasco took official possession of his post on April 16th of the same year.

The foregoing data differ considerably from the facts generally admitted, according to which Don José Ruiz came to Barcelona and took up his post at the beginning of October, in time to begin the academic year of 1895-1896.

How are we to understand the apparent contradiction of these two versions? As might be conjectured, and as Picasso himself has confirmed, Don José made a first journey to Barcelona by himself, in order to take up his post, and almost certainly asked for leave of absence immediately, for reasons of health. He took up his post on the last day of the period permitted, which was one month. This delay conceals another aspect of the problem. It was Don José's intention — or at least his desire — to exchange his Barcelona post for its counterpart in Palma, occupied by Manuel Rodríguez Codolá, who wanted to settle in Barcelona. But he was unable to effect this second exchange. Don José was tired; Majorca meant for him, not only returning to the Mediterranean, like Barcelona, but above all the "island of calm", a sort of pleasant retirement, enjoyed at the rhythm of provincial life. Barcelona, on the other hand, was a city in continuous ferment, and he would have many more pupils. And what would these Catalans be like?

3. The arrival. The evidence would appear to be that the Ruiz family arrived in Barcelona from Malaga about the middle of September of 1895, when Picasso was well into his fourteenth year. The family consisted of the father (Don José), the mother (Doña María) and the two children, Pablo and Lola.

Don José's brother, Don Salvador Ruiz Blasco, was Director of the Health Department of the port of Malaga, which gave his family and relatives material advantages in sea transport; and so, just as they had taken advantage of these conveniences to go to Vigo on the way to Corunna four years before, they now took a ship which went up along the Mediterranean coast from Malaga —via Almería, Alicante, Valencia, etc.— to Barcelona. Thus Picasso's first sight of Barcelona was from the sea: the heights of Montjuïc, with the city stretching out at its feet.

4. First home: No. 3, Calle Reina Cristina; No. 4, Calle Llauder. It would appear that the Ruiz family, on first arriving in Barcelona, stayed at a boarding-house near the port, possibly the one in which Don José had stayed on his previous visit. After that they spent some days in a flat on the ground floor of a large Neo-classical block popularly known as the "Arcades of En Xifré", but the light was so bad in this flat that they soon changed to one in the Calle Reina Cristina which also formed part of that block.

No. 3 in the Calle Reina Cristina is on the corner of the Calle Llauder, in which the same house occupies No. 4. This, I suppose, accounts for the confusion that has existed hitherto between these two homes, which were in fact only one. At first the entrance to the house usually used was the one in Calle Reina Cristina, but when an electric transformer was installed on the ground floor there (a fairly common improvement, at that time, in the more modern houses of Barcelona), it blocked this entrance and one of the staircases — which to this day, as can be seen, has no exit to the street. From then on the only address of the tenants of the flats was No. 4, Calle Llauder.

The flat occupied by Picasso's family was one on the second floor (really the fourth, since the house has a mezzanine and what is called a "main floor", as well as the numbered ones), and the windows of its rooms are those nearest the corner, both in the Calle Reina Cristina and in the Calle Llauder.

The whole block belonged then (and still belongs) to the Colom family.

The choice of this flat was dictated by Don José's need to be as close as possible to his work. To reach the Lonja, he had only to cross the Paseo de Isabel II. The Calle Reina Cristina and the Calle Llauder are at a stone's throw from the port, the former parallel to the wharves and the latter opening on to them. Picasso must surely have gone down to the port quite often — taken by his family or on his own account — and must soon have felt, through the still but restless water with its brackish smell, the urge to travel. The Estación de Francia, from which the trains for Paris left, was only a few steps away.

5. The entrance examination of the "Lonja" School. Around the "Lonja" School entrance examination a legend has been woven according to which Picasso, in twenty-four hours, completed the tests for which students were normally allowed a month. It is not that we do not consider Picasso capable of such a prodigy, and of even greater ones, but the fact is that the two drawings which have survived from this test bear different dates: the first is of

a) The house in the Calle Cristina, on the corner of the Calle Llauder (unpublished document).

b) The Columbus monument, at the end of the Ramblas, before the port....

1. Entrance examination drawing done at the Lonja School, Barcelona, 25th September 1895, 50.2 × 32.5 cm.
2. Entrance examination drawing done at the Lonja School, Barcleona, 30th September 1895.
   The Lonja: The centre of commercial transactions on the ground floor. School of Fine Arts on the second floor until very recently.

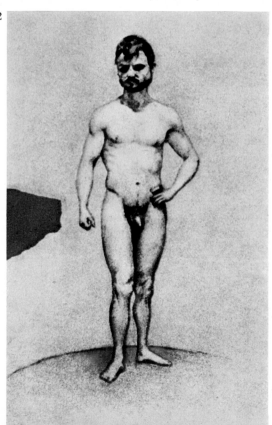

the 25th of September and the second of the 30th of September, of 1895.

Picasso, though his father almost certainly managed to have him excused from certain elementary exercises, apparently had to pass certain tests on different days. The remaining two show us the same model, one in a tunic and in profile, the other nude and full-face. In both the character is fixed with unerring precision. In the first Picasso may have seen a certain nobility, on account of the draping and the attitude needed to hold it up, but in the second version the man is, most

literally, naked. The first tells us of Picasso's facility for capturing beauty and exalting reality; the second, of his audacity in expressing reality stark naked, even ugly if necessary.

The "Lonja" entrance examination, at that time, consisted of three stages: 1: copying from prints (i.e., drawing what had already been drawn, what had already been reduced to two dimensions); 2: copying a plaster figure (an immobile model, which reminded one of the prints and acted as a bridge between them and the natural model); 3; exercises before a model or from nature. For this last test the students had to be at least twenty years old. Don José probably managed to have his son exempted from this condition and from the first two examinations. According to Manuel Pallarès, moreover, Picasso was exempted from these examinations because he had already passed them at the Da Guarda Institute in Corunna. Picasso was enrolled for the 1895-96 course in alphabetical order, his number being 108, under the name of Pablo Ruiz *Picano*.

6. Early drawings.

We have placed these two entrance examination drawings first because we know their dates and because they were done during Picasso's first days in our city and so, more or less officially, they serve us as a kind of inauguration of his Barcelona period. However, knowing the temperament of Picasso, his impetus and his impatience, we can hardly believe that there were no drawings prior to them, just after his arrival. This must have happened during his first contacts with the city. We must, therefore, count the two drawings of the Park of the Citadel among the earliest traces of his work in Catalonia; one a tenuously drawn sketch of the cascades of Gaudí, the other a study of a young lady with a parasol, watching the swans gliding across the lake; a pencil drawing, but with all the intensity of an etching.

7. "Picasso, copyist in the Museum".

In the course of research in the Barcelona Stock Exchange (the "Lonja"), the Mexican musician and musicologist Salvador Moreno has discovered an application signed by Picasso, and dated 5th October 1895, in which he notifies the director of the school that, "wishing to broaden his artistic knowledge in the Museum of the Establishment, he hereby requests per-

3. Pond in the Ciudadela Park. Barcelona, 1895. Pen and ink, 19.9 × 27.8 cm.

mission to copy in the said premises". This permission was granted to him until the end of January 1896, as we may read in the margin of the application itself. This document confirms the willingness, and even eagerness, to work shown by Pablo Ruiz Picasso when he first came to Barcelona. Don José, too, was probably anxious for his son to give these signs of reliability and diligence before his father's colleagues.

8. The first friend. It was in the "Lonja", at the beginning of the academic year,

a) The woman with the umbrella evokes a whole past...
b) Cléo de Mérode, one of the beauties of the period.
c and d) Two aspects of the Ramblas of Barcelona.

more precisely in the class of artistic anatomy taught by Tiberio Avila, that Picasso formed his first friendships. It would really be more proper to speak of his first friendship for, though there were other pupils in his course, he made friends at once with Manuel Pallarès, who, as we shall see, was to be one of the closest of his lifelong friends.

Manuel Pallarès i Grau was born in Horta de Sant Joan on March 6th; when they met, therefore, he was nineteen, six years older than Picasso. In Barcelona Pallarès lived in a boarding-house in the Calle de Escudellers. It may have been the fact that he was so far from his family that made the Ruiz household welcome him so cordially from the start. It was probably because he was older and so seemed to have more sense that Picasso's parents saw in him an ideal companion for their son and treated him like one of the family.

9. The city. As we have said, Barcelona in 1895 was a city which had already over half a million inhabitants and which had leaped over its own walls. In fact, the Plaza de Cataluña, where there were still houses and even mansions, and the "Riera d'en Malla" (Malla's Stream) —which is now the Calle Caspe, were more or less the limits of the old town, the principal artery of which was the Ramblas. The Gothic Quarter, thanks to the aging colours of its stones and façades, melted into the neighbouring districts, the streets of which, dark and narrow, paved with flagstones or cobblestones made to support wagons and horseshoes, seemed to be a poorer or, at least, less noble prolongation of their illustrious neighbour. These streets were — and those which survive still are — short, winding, full of surprises, even a little fearsome, and nearly all of them bear the medieval names of the trades that were carried on in them or the materials dealt in: we know them as "the Street of Straw, the Street of Glass, the Street of the Sandalmakers, the Street of the Silversmiths", etc.

In front of this kind of labyrinth, between the Plaza de Cataluña and the village of Gracia, the city had laid out a series of straight, wide, ordered streets, with the Paseo de Gracia in the centre; this was the "Eixampla" or Extension, the "Eixampla" which was such a source of pride to the people of Barcelona. Though the city had outgrown its walls, this modern district was, psychologically, a

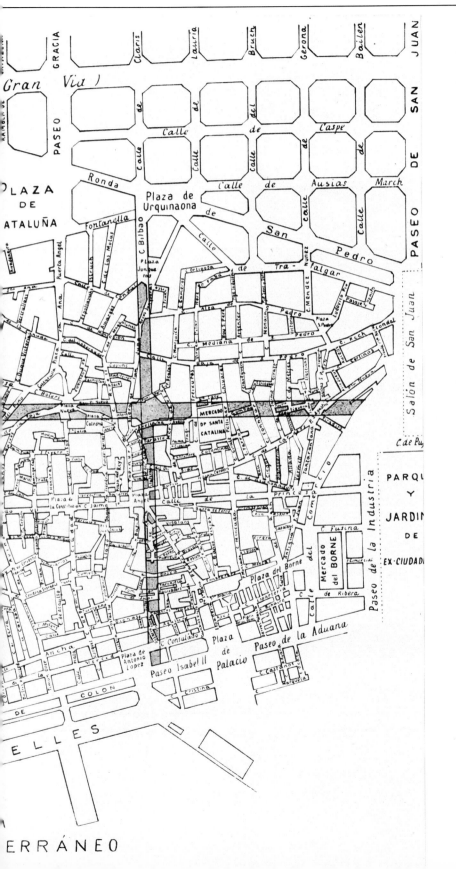

Partial plan of Barcelona, showing the old part of the city frequented by Picasso. The grey shading indicates the parts affected by town-planning changes.

kind of new world, a city-beyond-the-walls as it were: it represented a society which wanted to flee from all contact with dirt, with poverty, with its own immediate past; in short, a bourgeoisie which wanted to discount everything that had happened before its own social advancement gradually installed itself in this new district. Building work went on apace on the new lots thus formed. These clean streets, apparently so aseptic and lacking in character, were to be the image of that rising society.

We should say here and now that Picasso hardly ever moved out of the labyrinth of old Barcelona. As an adolescent he soon learned to wander round it rather as if he were searching for himself: the port, the "Lonja", the Gothic Quarter, the Paralelo (the Broadway of Barcelona at that time), the fishing quarter of the Barceloneta, Barcelona's "Chinatown"...

10. Time, place and problems. Picasso possessed, at heart, the profound gravity and the equally profound gaiety of the typical Andalusian; both qualities were so much a part of his character that he is often represented as an exclusively tragic type, incapable of the slightest irony, but

sometimes as a man who is completely banal, incapable of the least kind of seriousness. The years spent in Galicia, possibly on account of the countryside there and certain material difficulties, must have contributed to increasing the melancholic and introvert side of his character.

In Barcelona the first world in which Picasso found himself was that of the "Lonja". A feverish world, in which irony and mockery (this latter often rather mordant) were the order of the day. Barcelona had had a whole generation of talented humorists, some of whom were still alive: Albert Llanas, Peius Gener, Santiago Rusiñol... But all this wit was poured out in Catalan, in a language still strange to him. Perhaps, in spite of his native quickness, this new world disconcerted him a little at the beginning. But even in the middle of all the wit and badinage he must have seen at once the concern for art of all these people. The

4. Don José Ruiz Blasco, Picasso's father. Barcelona, 1896. Water-colour. Provincial Museum, Malaga.

great words of the day were: Paris, Impressionism, Art Nouveau, Symbolism. Rusiñol, Casas, Clarasó and Utrillo had made their first sortie to Paris in 1889. In Sitges they held what they called the "Art Nouveau Festivals" in 1892, 1893 and 1894. During the second of these Maeterlinck's "The Intruder" had been presented, in a translation by Pompeu Fabra, and during the third there was the famous procession to take the *Saint Peter* and the *Mary Magdalen* of El Greco, recently bought in Paris, to the museum of "Cau Ferrat" (Sitges), in an attempt to restore this painter to the place he deserved.

The great beauties of the period were Cléo de Mérode and Carolina de Otero.

In the newspapers of the time, the headlines concerned themselves with the death of Pasteur, including the corresponding chronicles and interpretations of his life and work, the removal of Odón de Buen from his post as Professor of Natural History in the University of Barcelona, followed by the usual student riots and manifestations and the no less usual repressions by the government; the performances of the Russian National Choir, who learned and sang such typical Catalan songs as *"El noi de la Mare"* and *"Sant*

4

Ramon", and the presentation of Sarah Bernhardt, who acted in the *Teatre Principal* from the 17th to the 23rd of October.

But the predominant note was that of the war in Cuba. This theme was in every issue, whether in news items trying to be realistic, comments which made a parade of intelligence or reports purporting to be impartial. But what was happening in Cuba? General Martínez Campos made inflammatory declarations, but there were already rumours that the United States

5. Doña María Picasso, Picasso's mother. Barcelona, 1895. Pastel, 50 × 39 cm.
Picasso Museum, Barcelona.

5

were secretly helping the insurgents, or the separatists as they were called.

Only one or two newspapers, like "El Diluvio" or "La Publicidad", dared to object to the government's policy. The others either approved of it or stayed cautiously on the side lines. "La Veu de Catalunya", which was then a weekly paper, made some attempt at clairvoyance: "The most fatal aspect of the war we are waging in Cuba is that it lacks moral force. All civilized states have modified their dealings with their colonies: all except Spain" (October 22nd 1895).

On October 25th, Picasso's fourteenth birthday, the papers carried the news that a train had raced into the station of Montparnasse, in Paris, at top speed and had crashed down into the street two floors below. It was at the same time a symbol of progress and of the terror that progress still inspired in the minds of many.

Another word of the moment was anarchism. Barcelona was then, and for many decades would continue to be, the anarchist capital *par excellence*, the place where the anarchistic forces, then in the ascendant all over Europe, were to have, socially speaking, an unquestionable pre-

Photograph of Picasso, taken on his arrival in Barcelona, in 1895.

ponderance among the working classes and sometimes in the city as a whole, to a point where they were absolute masters. Jaume Brossa had been the champion and the definer of the Catalan kind of anarchism, before Francesc Ferrer founded the Modern School and the Revolutionary Institute, in 1901.

During the second Art Nouveau festival, this "new art" had been defined by Rusiñol in terms that might have been used by a *poète maudit*.

Nietzsche, then only considered the singer of the dark, wild forces of human nature, was the greatest name of the moment, and very soon Maragall himself was to translate his works into Catalan. This year, in fact, saw the apparition of the *Poems* of Maragall, a work of capital importance in the history of modern Catalan poetry.

It should also be noted that towards the end of 1892, on the occasion of the fourth centenary of the discovery of America by Columbus, Barcelona was flooded with pre-Columbian idols and statues of all sorts, some authentic but others manufactured locally. The most outstanding of all these objects were two totems that came from a Red Indian tribe in Canada. The two totems stayed in Barcelona for a long time and must have attracted great attention among the local artists, many of whom had worked in the production of imitation figures. I have been convinced for a long time now that it was memories of this art, rather than negro art, that must have influenced Picasso years later when he was painting *Les demoiselles d'Avignon*, and that it was the same kind of memories that produced the work done by Torres García in his last period.

11. First works. The subject of Picasso's first drawings and pictures in Barcelona, apart from those already mentioned, was the reality that most immediately surrounded him: his family. His father, his mother and his sister were often his models, consciously or not, repeatedly caught in various attitudes.

One of the earliest is the water colour of his father, covered with a striped blanket and wearing a nightcap, which was sent as a Christmas present in 1895 to Don Antonio Muñoz Degrain, in Malaga, and which is now in the Provincial Museum of Fine Arts in that city.

From the beginning of 1896 is the bust of his mother in right profile, in which he

6. Manuel Pallarès, the first friend. Barcelona, 1895. Oil on cardboard, 35.3 × 25 cm. Private collection, Barcelona.

6

7. Manuel Pallarès painting. Barcelona, 1895. Pen and ink, 29.5 × 23.8 cm. Private collection, Barcelona.

8. Manuel Pallarès in profile. Barcelona, 1895. Pen and ink, 26 × 19.5 cm. Dedicated and signed in 1933. Private collection, Barcelona.

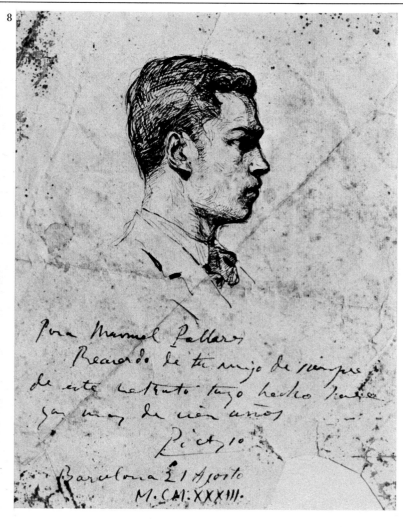

9. The first communion. Barcelona, 1896. Oil on canvas, 164×116 cm. Picasso Museum, Barcelona.

10. The altar boy. Barcelona, 1896. Oil on canvas, 76×50 cm. Sala Collection, Barcelona.

Offering to the Blessed Virgin, by José Garnelo, one of the teachers at the Lonja. Published in "La Ilustración Artística" on 9-III-1896 (unpublished document).

10

11. Head of bearded man (a model at the Lonja). Barcelona, 1896. Oil on canvas,
    28.5×36 cm. Private collection (unpublished).

11

12. The man with the long beard. Barcelona. 1896. Oil. Formerly in the Maurice
Chevalier Collection, Marnes-la-Coquette (France).

12

seems to have been mainly concerned with catching a likeness, an aim in which he surely succeeded. Another work still extant from this early Barcelona period is a portrait in oils of his friend Manuel Pallarès.

A water-colour of a negro draped in white — a kind of Othello — seems to have been painted from one of the "Lonja" models.

A picture which was certainly painted from one of these models is the *Man with the long beard*, formerly in the collection of Maurice Chevalier. As regards the style and composition this picture is still akin to the works done in Corunna, though with a more academic accent.

A *Head of a bearded man*, reproducing another of the Lonja models, seems to have had much the same type of inspiration. I think it is not too far-fetched to see in these two works the possible influence of Antoni Caba, at that time director of the Lonja school and professor of drawing and colouring. Caba was a man much feared and admired, and some of his paintings are really too sensitive to be considered strictly academic.

The man with the long beard is already a museum piece, for it possesses all the qualities then demanded of works for such places. It is a painting based on "chiaroscuro", in which the limpness of the beard is contrasted with the firmness of the muscle and the strength of the forehead, though by this we do not mean that these three different qualities alter the rhythm of the brushstrokes in the least.

The Picassos of Picasso, by David Douglas Duncan, possesses, among other virtues, that of revealing to us several works of Picasso's first period in Barcelona, among them *The flight into Egypt* and

Picasso painted by a fellow-pupil of the Lonja called Rius.

13.   Self-portrait of Picasso as an eighteenth-century gentleman. Barcelona, 1896-1897. Oil on canvas, 55.8 × 46 cm. Picasso Museum, Barcelona.

14.   Self-portrait of Picasso with his hair beginning to grow again. Barcelona, 1896-1897. Lead pencil.

13

14

The Almoina. In *The lover's flight* we see, for the first time, Picasso's interest in theatrical subjects, for the scene takes place on a stage and, apart from pictorial veracity, Picasso wanted to convey the dramatic truth to us. On theatrical subjects there is also a water colour of the same year (1896), in which there are two women, one seated and the other standing, in attitudes clearly of the theatre.

12. The First Communion.   Almost from the moment he first came to Barcelona,

Picasso was painting in two different styles: one a formal, academic manner and the other absolutely free, daring in execution and concept.

His outstanding works in the first manner are *The altar boy* and *The first communion*, which were most probably done consecutively during the first three months of 1896, since the second was shown at the Fine Arts Exhibition of Barcelona, which opened on 23rd April of that year. For the painting of this composition his models were his sister Lola, as

15. Work sheet, showing Don José in the centre and around him the words "Distinguished, Failed...". Barcelona, 1896-1897.

15

the first communicant, and a friend of the Ruiz Family called Vilches. The latter's son, apparently, was the model for *The altar boy*, in which work, perhaps through the influence of Mas i Fontdevila (as J. F. Ràfols has pointed out), the prevailing tones are white and red, symbolizing purity and love respectively.

The first communion was painted in the studio one of his teachers, José Garnelo, had in the Plaza de la Universidad. José Garnelo was a painter of religious and historical subjects, for the painting of which he needed to set up in his studio a whole stage setting, with many sitters and "extras", dressed up in whatever costumes the scene required, Picasso told me that on one occasion he had seen in that studio a complete grotto of Lourdes, with the Blessed Virgin, Bernardette and all.

In his review of the Fine Arts Exhibition, published in the "Diario de Barcelona" on 25th May 1896, Miquel i Badia wrote: "*The First Communion*, by Pablo Ruiz Picasso, is the work of a neophyte, in which we can see a certain feeling in the principal characters and some parts firmly outlined."

But these two works, like the slightly later *Science and Charity*, were really a

34

mask hiding the true Picasso, who, when left to his own devices, executed an infinite number of works which, though apparently less important, are of much greater significance to my way of thinking from the creative point of view, in the daring of their concept and their liveliness. They are usually tiny pictures, works done on stray pieces of paper or board that he picked up here, there and everywhere to serve as vehicles for his overflowing inspiration.

The most interesting of these works, because of the modernity of their execution, are a few self-portraits and some compositions that verge on the abstract.

13. Portraits and self-portraits. From that same year, 1896, dates the first photograph we have of Picasso in Barcelona, which as far as the spirit of the character is concerned coincides with those three pictures so formally painted during the same period. It represents an obedient, rather irresolute boy. The personality of the subject seems constrained, as if he felt uncomfortable in the suit — which, indeed, sits just as falsely on him as does the one he is wearing in a portrait of him painted by a fellow pupil at the

Lonja called Riu (or Rius). In both Picasso is shown with his head shaven, which is the way he usually wore it at this time. In contrast to these, however, there is a *Self-portrait* painted in the same year in which he has painted himself as an eighteenth-century gentleman. Possibly the close-cropped image that he saw in his looking-glass did not wholly please him, so that he made use — possibly for the first time — of his enormous facility for transforming mere persons into personages and so painted himself in this metamorphosis. Indeed, the most characteristic feature of this *Self-portrait* is its magnificent head of white hair. It is one of the first signs to be seen of the young Picasso breaking free. Other self-portraits of the period chronicle, almost step by step, the growth of his hair into what was to be the definitive mop, dangling forelock and all.

14. New friendships. Among the fellow students at the Lonja, apart from Pallarès, with whom Picasso seems to have made friends quite quickly, we might mention Joaquim Bas i Gich, Josep Cardona and Francisco Bernareggi.

a) Note by Manuel Pallarès confirming the situation of the studio in the Calle de la Plata (unpublished document).
b) The flat roof of the studio in the Calle de la Plata, today.
c) The Calle de Canvis Nous.
d) N.º 3, Calle de la Merced.

c

b

a

El estudio que Picasso tuvo en la calle de la Plata y que yo
compartía con él, estaba situado en la casa número 4 (cuatro) de
dicha calle, o sea, entrando por el Paseo de Colón a mano izquierda.
El estudio se hallaba en el último rellano del edificio, desde don-
teníamos acceso a los terrados.

Manuel Pallarés
Barcelona, 29 de diciembre de 1971.

d

We also know that Picasso, with Pallarès, frequently visited the *café chantant*
called the "Edèn Concert", most probably
to draw the girls who sang there, who
would naturally be more atractive than
the exclusively male models at the Lonja.
It would appear, too, that it was at this
café chantant that he first made the
acquaintance of the Soto brothers and the
Reventós brothers.

In the list of pupils enrolled at the
school that year, moreover, we find such
names as Torné Esquius, a notable painter
and draughtsman who is now largely

forgotten, and Ricard Urgell, son of the famous painter Modest Urgell.

15. The bomb in the "Calle de Canvis Nous". 1896, in the social sense, was the year of the bomb in the "Calle de Canvis Nous". The city was just beginning to forget the night of the bomb in the Liceo (Barcelona's Opera House), eighteen months before, when it was shaken by this bomb, which exploded on June 7th, just after the procession of "Santa María del Mar", and which killed seven people. Not long afterwards — July 14th — the papers carried the news of the attempted assassination, in the Bois de Boulogne, of the President of the French Republic, Félix Faure. Anarchism was certainly at its height in Europe.

In August a law for the suppression of anarchism was proclaimed in Madrid, but some commentators feared that the remedy might be worse than the disease.

16. New home. Almost certainly before the beginning of the second academic year, the Ruiz family moved from the Calle Llauder to a third-floor flat in the Calle de la Merced (Number 3), also situated in the vinicity of the "Lonja", where they were to remain long after Picasso left Barcelona.

17. "Lonja" School of Fine Arts, 1896-1897. After having spent the summer in Malaga, Picasso enrolled in the Lonja again, for his second academic year in Barcelona, most probably to please his father. He was entered with the number 76 and under the name of Pablo Ruiz y Picasso. He was to use the school occasionally, to draw one or other of their new models; but there can be no doubt that these exercises merely served to prove to him that he could follow that way only up to a certain point, which he had already reached, and that if he persisted in that way he would simply be repeating himself.

This disaccord with his situation and, consequently, with his father, seems to be reflected in one of those drawings done in 1897, real fields of work, lined on all sides with sketches of hands, faces, arms and legs, in one of which we see Don José, sitting with his hands in his pockets and his legs crossed and, around the figure, written in what seems to be his writing, the world *Failed* (4 times) and *Distinguished* (6 times), which help us to under-

Paternina: *The Mother's Visit* (unpublished document).

16. First rough sketch for "Science and Charity". Barcelona, 1896-1897. Drawing on the back of the portrait of J. Vidal Ventosa, 47×27.5 cm. Picasso Museum, Barcelona.

17. Final preparatory sketch for "Science and Charity". Barcelona, 1896-1897. Oil. Formerly in the Picasso Collection.

18. Science and Charity. Barcelona, 1896-1897. Oil on canvas, 197×249 cm. Picasso Museum, Barcelona.

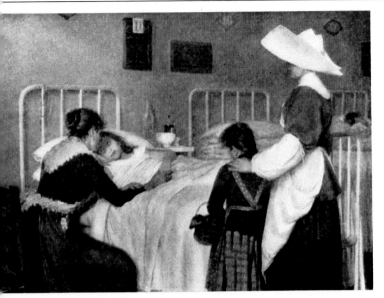

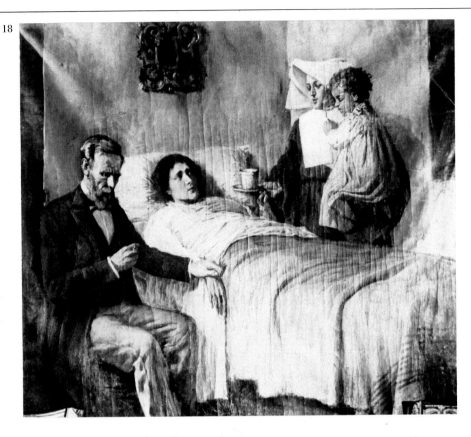

18

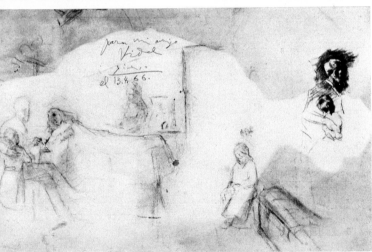

stand the argument that was going on between father and son.

But Don José, persuaded of the precocity of his son and of his independent character, finally decided, surely encouraged to do so by his wife, to rent a studio for the boy in order to accelerate the development of his personality.

18. The first studio. A studio of his own, for a boy of fourteen, is at once an incentive and a peril; but Pablo's parents knew that he had a good friend, Pallarès, who would often be there. The studio, on

19. Solei (a model at the Lonja). Academic study. Barcelona, 1896. Conté pencil, 47 × 19.5 cm.
20. Solei (a model at the Lonja). Free interpretation. Barcelona, 1897. India ink, 30 × 20 cm.
21. Head of a boy (a model at the Lonja). Barcelona, 1897. Oil on strong paper, 29 × 23.5 cm. Formerly in the Picasso Collection.

19   20   21

the top landing of a house at Number 4 in the Calle de la Plata was half-way between his parent's house and the "Lonja" and so his father would have to pass it every day.

A studio, for an adolescent who feels his vocation with overwhelming force, is almost like a first love: all his illusions meet and crystallize in it. When Picasso, at the age of fourteen or fifteen, crossed the threshold of that house and passed under the arch of the vestibule to go upstairs to the top landing, he must have felt a kind of strange satisfaction; all his future must have seemed to grow, potentially, before his eyes in this place. His personality must have been strengthened by this studio. Here began the battle with life.

19. Science and Charity. This concession of his father's, however, cannot have been

22. Tavern interior. Barcelona, 1897. Oil, 19 × 24 cm. O'Hana Gallery, London.

23. Silhouette of "Don José". Barcelona, 1897. Oil on canvas, 19 × 14 cm. Formerly in the Picasso Collection.

23

nion. The principal result of all these circumstances was *Science and Charity.* Before starting work on the canvas itself, Picasso did numerous preparatory sketches, and it is in these rather than in the finished work that we catch a glimpse of Picasso's genius and unceasing dynamism. The characters move and adopt different postures, disappear or are transformed, before they are given their definitive attitudes. For Picasso, that eternal ally of life in art, it must surely have been an effort to imprison them in "poses" and to submit, for his own part, to such a static vision.

The subject, and the two terms — *science* and *charity* — used to describe it, form a whole programme and express, very synthetically, the mentality and aspirations of the age. It is difficult not to see in this the influence of the painter's father, for at the Lonja school, and in Barcelona in general, don José was to be long remembered as an extraordinarily kindly man. At that time modern science was making its great entrance into the world; in conjunction with charity it might become an incalculable force for good. That, at least, is the postulate hinted at in this work. To illustrate it we

made without certain conditions. For his only son Don José wanted all that he could have desired for himself and had not been able to achieve: to be an eminent, recognized painter, in the Spanish academic tradition and in all the official circles. He certainly could not imagine that his son might ever be *more* than that. In renting the studio his intention was that Pablo should prepare to compete in the official exhibitions of the academic salons, as he had already done with *The first commu-*

24. Self-portrait. Barcelona, 1898. Conté pencil, 32 × 24.7 cm. Formerly in the
Picasso Collection.

24

are shown a sick woman lying in bed, while the doctor (science), sitting beside her, is taking her pulse, and a nun (charity) on the other side of the bed holds up the woman's little son. This meant that Picasso had to have a truckle bed set up, on which they laid a poor woman who had been begging recently in the district with her child in her arms. Don José himself was the model for the doctor, while the sick woman's child (the beggar's own child, in fact) was held up by a nun who was, it seems, a young boy dressed up.

This great composition seems to have taken its inspiration from a picture by Paternina (a well-known Spanish painter at the turn of the century) which was shown at the Fine Arts Exhibition of Barcelona in 1896, and which Picasso must therefore have seen. Paternina's picture was entitled *The mother's visit*. It is not only the subject that is similar (Picasso had at first intended to call his picture *The visit to the sick woman*), but even some elements of the composition too, though Picasso gradually changed his work to avoid too literal a resemblance to Paternina's picture. Where the two compositions are most alike is in their sentimental motif. In Paternina's work the

subject is a poor sick girl being visited by her mother at the hospital, while a nun also hovers in attendance. But Picasso accentuated this dramatic aspect still more. In *Science and Charity* the woman — equally sick and poor — has not even got her mother to keep her company. Nor is she being cared for in the hospital, but in her own wretched room, where she is visited by the doctor and by a Sister of Charity who is holding up the little boy she cannot look after herself.

Science and Charity was painted in the studio in the Calle de la Plata, but we do not know exactly when; it was probably between May 1896 and February or March 1897. It would seem more logical to conjecture, provisionally at any rate, that Picasso started on this task on his return from Malaga, after having been "admonished" by his family and told that he should try to paint a work worthy of "a great painter". It might also be supposed that in order to avoid hurting the feelings of José Garnelo — who was, after all, his father's colleague — Picasso finished his first academic year in Barcelona working in that teacher's studio, and that Don José rented the studio in the Calle de la Plata for him as from the autumn of 1896. This

25. Yoked horse. Barcelona, June 1898. Drawing in coloured pencils, 25 × 28 cm.
    Formerly in the Picasso Collection.

would place the painting of the picture at some time in the last three months of 1896 or the first three of 1897.

Science and Charity was sent to the National Fine Arts Exhibition of Madrid in 1897, where it obtained an Honourable Mention, and later to the Provincial Exhibition of Malaga, at which it was awarded a Gold Medal. For many years the picture hung in the hall of Don Salvador Ruiz Blasco's house in the Alameda, in Malaga, and on his death it returned to Picasso's family home in Barcelona.

It is no secret, however, that Picasso in later years declared to Kahnweiler that he disagreed with the formal spirit of those compositions of his that had been painted for such exhibitions.

We must not forget that, when all this was happening, Picasso was only fourteen or fifteen years old, and that though his precocity led him to make friends with boys who were almost always older than he, he was still only an adolescent who felt at times the urge to get up to all the tricks of a boy of his age.

And so, with his friend Pallarès, he sometimes used to throw pebbles down on the passers-by from the roof of the house in the Calle de la Plata. And at Carnival time one year the two friends dressed up as women, while another year they wore Moorish costume, etc.

20. Historical context. In Spain at this time ill feeling over the war in Cuba was on the increase, and the situation was hardly improved by the insurrection in the Philippines. General Martínez Campos had been replaced by General Weyler, until then Captain General of Catalonia.

44

a) The mountain of Santa Bárbara, with the convent of San Salvador at its foot.
b) The torrent in which Picasso was on the point of drowning.
c) The Passes of the Maestrat, with the "Ullals de Morago" in the background.
d) The Rock under which Picasso and Pallarès may have sheltered.
e) General view of Horta de Ebro.
f) The "Mas del Quiquet", among the Passes.
g) Salvadoret, with the donkey, at the Passes.
h) "Can Tafetans", seat of the Pallarès family, at N.º 11, Calle de Grau.

26. Houses in Horta de Ebro. Horta de Ebro, 1898. Oil on canvas, 27 × 39 cm. Formerly in the Picasso Collection.

27. Shepherd courting a shepherdess at the Ports del Maestrat (sketch for "Idyll"). Horta de Ebro, 1898. Conté pencil, 15.5 × 21.5 cm.

28. A tree at the Ports del Maestrat. Horta de Ebro, 1898. Conté pencil, 24.8 × 16.5 cm.

29. Manuel Pallarès at the Ports del Maestrat. Horta de Ebro, 1898. Conté pencil, 24.6 × 16 cm.

30. Shepherd boy at the Ports del Maestrat. Horta de Ebro, 1898. Conté pencil, 32 × 24.5 cm.

31. Notes of sheep at the Ports del Maestrat. Horta de Ebro, 1898. Drawing in coloured pencil, 28 × 25 cm.

27

29

30

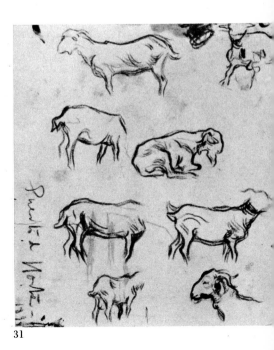

31

32. Portrait of Josefa Sebastià Membrado. Horta de Ebro, November 1898.
33. Procession of women to the hermitage of Sant Salvador. Horta de Ebro, 1898.
   Oil and pastel on canvas, 60 × 71 cm. Formerly in the Picasso Collection.

Meanwhile Barcelona was expanding and was anxious to take on the appearance of a modern city. In February a Commission was set up to study the city's rights to the land in the Plaza de Cataluña.

21. Last works. A change of attitude appears to be reflected in the last works of this period of Picasso's residence in Barcelona, among which I should mention the *Café interior*, done with very free brushwork. A tiny *Portrait of Don José* (18.5 × 14 cm.) shows that the pupil has become a master.

This increasing freedom, which has never been lacking in the works done on his own account, finally made itself felt even in the last canvases painted using the Lonja models, as we may see in the *Head of a boy* which seems to mark the completion of this stage.

Picasso probably stayed in Barcelona until about the middle of July 1897, when Don José would have finished with his teaching duties for that second academic year, before going to spend the summer in Malaga with the rest of his family.

22. The "4 Gats". But shortly before his departure — on June 12th 1897, to be

34. Peasant woman, with Horta de Ebro in the background. 1898. Pencil and pastel, 31.5 × 48 cm.

35. Portrait of Josep Cardona. Barcelona, 1899 (1898, according to Zervos and Alex Maguy). Oil on canvas, 100 × 63 cm. Private collection.

36. Portrait of Angel F. de Soto. 1899. Oil on canvas, 62 × 50 cm. Leonesco Collection, Buenos Aires.

35

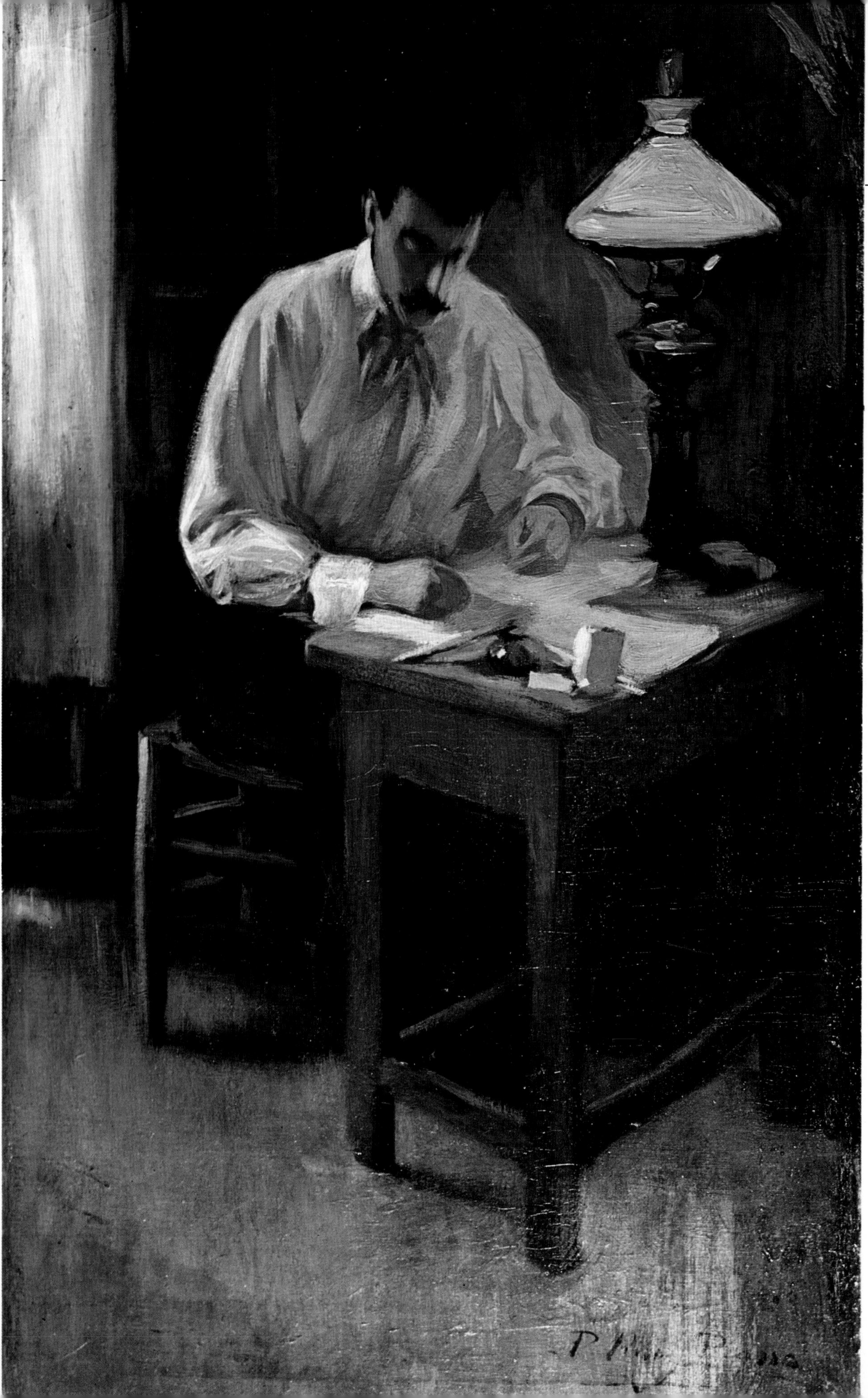

36

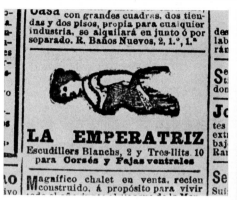

37

precise — the famous establishment known as the "4 Gats" opened its doors.

This blend of café, beer-garden and cabaret owed its name to memories of Rodolphe Salis' celebrated "Chat Noir" in Paris, but also to a popular Catalan saying, "We're only four cats", meaning that there is nobody, or hardly anybody, present in a place or at a meeting.

The premises were on the ground floor of a house on the corner of the Calle de Montesión and the Pasaje del Profeta, built in neo-Gothic style by the architect Puig i Cadafalch. The public part was elongated, with two arches at one end and five along the side. Inside, the walls had a dado of Valencian tiles one metre high. The ceiling had bare beams, some of them artificial, to add character to the general effect. Between the dado and the ceiling the walls were covered with pictures, drawings, plates and all sorts of bric-à-brac. There were dark-stained wooden chairs and tables, and wrought-iron chandeliers. In a prominent position was a picture painted by Ramon Casas, showing himself and Pere Romeu riding a tandem. At the end of the century this great panel was replaced by another, also painted by Casas, showing him driving a motor-car, at that time the ultimate in daring modernity. Pere Romeu was the founder and "inn-keeper" of the "4 Gats", and Miquel Utrillo and Ramon Casas were his literary and artistic advisers respectively. Rusiñol was from the start, and continued to be, one of the authorities of the house. At the end of the bar the premises widened into a room intended to be used for shadow plays, under the direction of Miquel Utrillo. At a later period there were also puppet shows, presented by Juli Pi.

The poster announcing the opening of the "4 Gats" began as follows: "To all persons of good taste, to the citizens from

38. Art Nouveau painter, surrounded by onlookers, in a Barcelona street. Barcelona, around 1900. Charcoal drawing.

39. Flamenco dancer. Barcelona, around 1901. Pastel. Reproduced in the last number of "Pèl & Ploma", Barcelona, December 1903.

40. "A dirty old man". Barcelona, 1899. Charcoal and water-colour, 32 × 24.8 cm. (unpublished in colour).

39

40

41. Portrait of Lola, Picasso's sister. Barcelona, 1899. Sepia, 23.1×17 cm.

42. The angel of death. Inspired by the wounded in the Cuban war. Barcelona, 1899. Water-colour and Conté pencil, 45.5×30 cm. Solomon Guggenheim Museum, New York.

41

42

43

river to river (Barcelona lies between two rivers, the Besós and the Llobregat), to those who feel the need to regale not only their body but also their spirit..."

Shortly afterwards (10th July) the first exhibition was held at the "4 Gats", showing works by Casas, Rusiñol, Utrillo, Bonnin, Nonell, Canals, Mir and Pitxot.

"Two new painters are making their debut at the '4 Gats' gallery," wrote A. Opisso, the art critic of "La Vanguardia". "Torrent, with an extremely personal work, *The Courtyard*, and Espert, with some cloudy studies of heads..."

As we can see, Picasso's name does not appear at all. Was this one of the reasons why, after the holidays in Malaga with his family, he decided to spend the next academic year in Madrid? He did come first to Barcelona, however, and left for Madrid, most probably around the end of October, to enrol in the Royal Academy of San Fernando.

23. "Horta de Ebro" (Horta de Sant Joan). But Picasso returned to Barcelona about the middle of May, 1898, in very bad physical shape and, what was even worse for him, having achieved practically nothing positive during his stay in Ma-

44

45. "La Musclera" (The Mussel-house). Barcelona, 1899 or 1900. Oil on canvas, 48.5×48 cm. Formerly in the Picasso Collection.
46. Gypsy girl in front of "La Musclera". Barcelona, 1900 or 1901. Pastel, 44.5×60 cm.

drid. This return to Barcelona was also a return to his first friend, for very soon afterwards, most probably on or about St. John's Day (June 24th), he went with Manuel Pallarès to the latter's family house in Horta de Ebro.

Horta de Ebro is a village in the Terra Alta district of the province of Tarragona, at about sixteen kilometres from Gandesa on the road to Aragon. Situated on a hill at about five hundred metres above sea level, it was formerly known as Puigventós de la Figuereta, and on its escutcheon it still has a fig tree ("Figuereta" in Catalan means "little fig tree").

Since the eighteenth century it has been known as Horta (possibly a corruption of Forta). According to Picasso, it was Pallarès who, perhaps to distinguish it from the district of Horta in Barcelona, re-christened the village Horta de Ebro, which is why I have adopted that form here. The official name of Horta de Sant Joan dates from 1919.

According to what Manuel Pallarès himself told me, he and Picasso took the train as far as Tortosa, where they were met by Manuel's elder brother, Josep, with a mule which they used in turns for the rest of the journey.

The home of the Pallarès family was at No. 11 in the Calle de Grau, in the upper

47. The divan. Barcelona, 1901. Charcoal, pastel and coloured pencils on
     varnished paper, 25 × 29 cm. Picasso Museum, Barcelona.

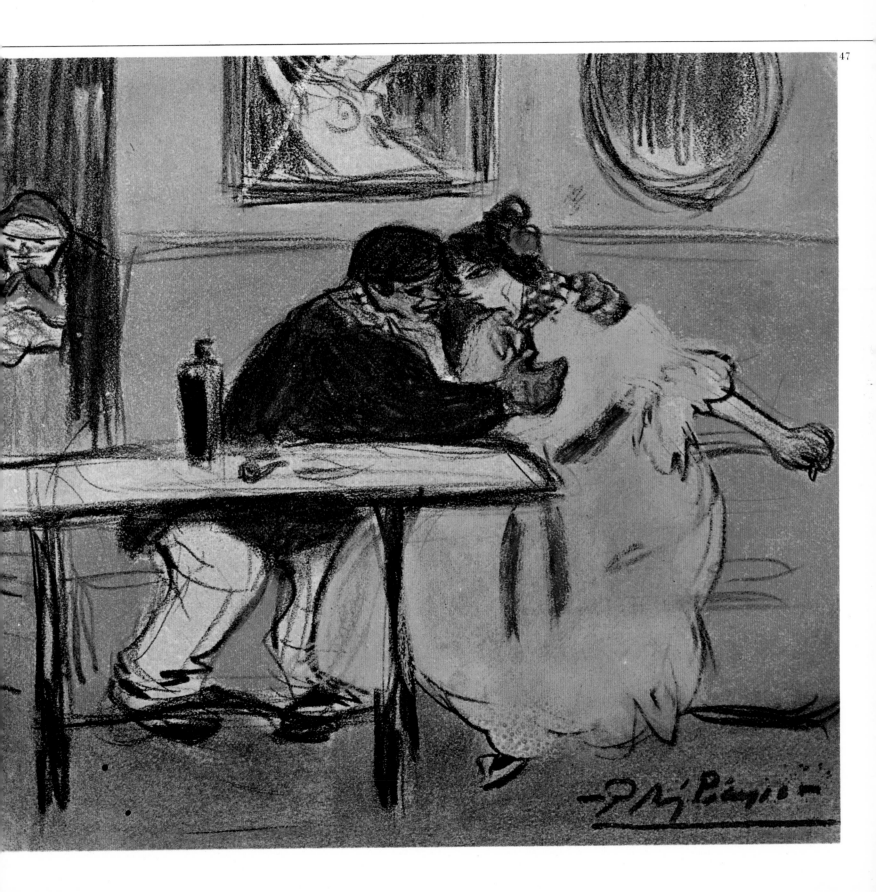

47

48. Manola. Barcelona, 1899 (?). Pastel, 44.5×21 cm. Roh-Rey Collection, Geneva (Switzerland).

49. Portrait of Sebastià Junyer-Vidal: "Sebastianus III König". Barcelona, around 1899. Lead pencil, coloured pencils and water-colour on varnished paper, 21×16 cm. Picasso Museum, Barcelona (unpublished in colour).

50. Lola Ruiz Picasso, the artist's sister. Barcelona, 1899. Charcoal and coloured pencils on paper, 44×29 cm. Picasso Museum, Barcelona.

50

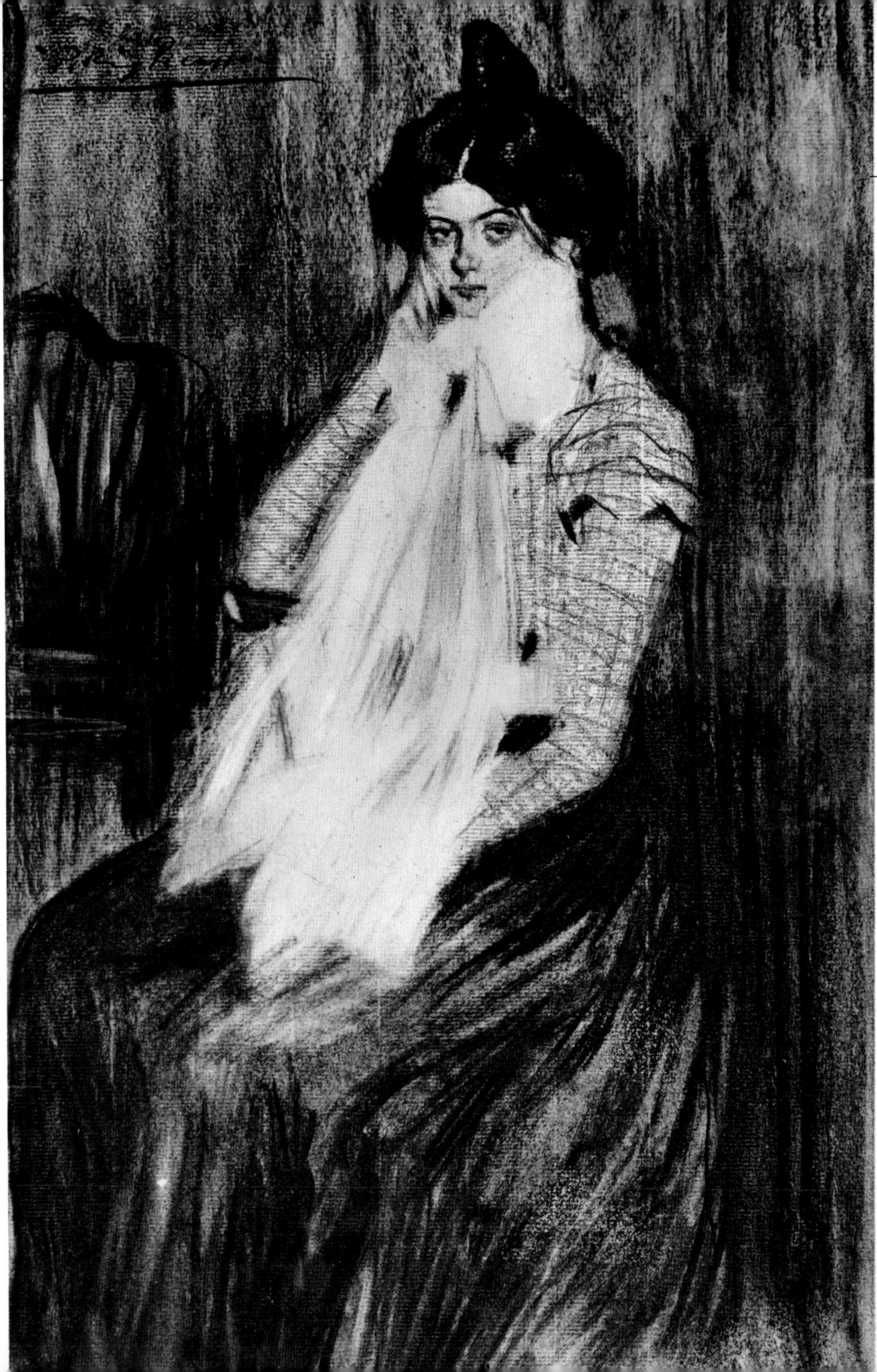

58

51. Design for a poster announcing the 1900 Carnival. Barcelona. Gouache and
    Conté pencil, 49 × 31.5 cm. Reverse of No. 52. Formerly in the Picasso
    Collection.

52. Design for a poster announcing the 1900 Carnival. Barcelona. Gouache and
    Conté pencil, 49 × 31.5 cm. Obverse of No. 51. Formerly in the Picasso
    Collection.

53. View of the roofs around the studio at No. 17 in the Riera de Sant Joan.
Barcelona, 1900. Pastel, 37.8 × 50.9 cm.

Picasso, with Casagemas (on the right) and M. F. de Soto (in the middle), on
the flat roof of No. 3, Calle de la Merced.

53

part of the village, which at that time ended in a sort of castle or tower. At the time of Picasso's visit to Horta the Pallarès family consisted of three brothers, Josep, Manuel and Salvador, and one sister, Carme.

Apparently Pallarès and Picasso did not stay long in the village after their arrival. When the hot weather came, they explored the surroundings, places like San Salvador, at the foot of the mountain of Santa Bárbara, which they climbed several times. Half-way up there was a cave where they stayed some days. But this urge to live in the midst of nature and to escape from the heat gradually turned into a protracted stay in a cave in the "Ports" or Passes. The Passes of the Maestrat are a region of imposing mountains, outstanding among which are the "Ullals" (Eyeteeth) de Morago, awesome in name and appearance, embedded there as if in the jaws of hell.

Salvadoret, as the youngest of the Pallarès family was called, accompanied his brother and Picasso as far as the Passes, with a donkey which carried the provisions and the painting gear and canvases. From there on the two friends continued on foot, with all their impedimenta on their backs. It was around here that Picasso, as they were climbing along the slippery rocks on the banks of a mountain stream, fell headlong with all his baggage and Pallarès, who was in front, was just in time to catch hold of him and rescue him and his gear. Picasso had a real fright, for he couldn't swim and the stream was deep. Ever since then, whenever they met, Picasso would say to Pallarès: "I'll never forget that you saved my life".

The cave where they installed themselves is really a big rock sticking out from the side of the mountain, which forms a kind of projecting roof under which one can shelter. There they made two beds of herbs and straw, but when it rained, as there was an open crack in one side of the rock, the rain came in. Picasso and Pallarès went there to paint a couple of pictures, but such a strong wind arose that it broke their stretchers and cords, and they had to do as best they could putting the canvases on new stretchers.

It is surely to this stay in the cave that we owe that series of images of various trees, caught by the eye of Picasso, those sketches of a shepherd courting a shepherdess (when he began the picture, it was called "*Idyll*"), and that little shepherd lad, alone, leaning on his staff...

Their day in the Passes began with a shower of cold water, as much to wake them up as to wash them, and it ended with their lighting a big fire to make their supper and to talk for a long time beside it before going to bed.

Not very far from the cave is the "Mas" (Farm) "del Quiquet", which is where their food came from. Sometimes, too, they were visited — always at the exact time arranged — by Salvadoret, who brought them, on his donkey, their letters and provisions and the working material they needed. It must also have been Salvadoret who brought them news of the outside world and who, one fine day in August (the Treaty of Paris was signed on the 13th), told them of the end of the war in Cuba. The nightmare was over.

The contemporary history of Spain is usually considered to have begun as from this date when the nation left off dreaming of past glories to face its present reality. It seems more than paradoxical — I nearly said providential — that Picasso should have been reborn, so to speak, at this time, when he left Madrid and the copying of the great masters of

a) Interior of the "4 Gats".

b) Interior of the "4 Gats", with Angel and Mateo F. de Soto (left and right, respectively), both wearing bowler hats. In the background, Pere Romeu.

c) Exterior of the building which housed the "4 Gats".

d) Poster announcing the opening of the "4 Gats".

55. Drawing showing the entrance to the puppet theatre at the "4 Gats". Barcelona, 1899. Lead pencil.

56. Lady sitting at a table in the "4 Gats". Barcelona, 1899. Lead pencil.

57. Interior of the "4 Gats". The man at the table represents the poet Nogueras-Oller. Barcelona, 1899. Oil, 41×28 cm. Simon M. Jaglom Collection, New York.

a

55

b

56

c

Als

A les persones
de bon gust,
als ciutadans
de riu a riu,
als que, en/
semps de l'aliment pel seu
cos, necessiten alimentar l'es/
perit,

En **Pere Romeu**
els fa avinent que en el car/
rer de Montesion, entrant
per la plaça de Santa Ana,
segona casa a mà esquerra,
die dotze del més de Juny estarà obert
oliment tant propi per l'espargiment dels
n nutrit de bones coses per complaure l

tal estada és hostal pels desganats, és
de caliu pels que sentin l'anyorança de
és museu pels que busquin lleminadures
ima; és taverna y emparrat pels que
ombra dels pampols, y de l'essencia es/
a del rahim; és gotica cerveseria pels
ats del Mort, y pati d'Andalusia pels
rs del mig-die; és casa de curació pels
del nostre segle, y cau d'amistat y har/
pels que entrin a roplugar-se sota la
de la casa.

o tindran penediment d'haver vingut, y si
si no vénen.

d

57

the past, in order to strengthen his links with the primitive forces of the country...

At the end of the summer or the beginning of the autumn, the two friends returned to the village. Picasso's health had quite recovered, and he was happy there. He liked to mingle with the locals; to watch the locksmith, the harness maker, the sandal maker or the farmer at their jobs. After having let the forces of nature raise him, almost literally, from the feet up, as though he were a tree or a plant, he now took pleasure in learning the crafts of these men, the sons of that region: and so he learnt how to make a noose, how to saddle a mule, and so on... A series of sketches, unfinished and untouched, bear witness to his interest in this multiple human activity. Hence that phrase of his, which has become world-famous: "Everything I know, I learnt in Horta de Ebro". And indeed Picasso was later to make good use of these manual skills at various times in the course of his life...

We must also say that it was here that he learnt his good Catalan, more alive than that of Barcelona, which had deteriorated so much at that time.

Of this stay in Horta few important compositions remain. Some, we know, were destroyed, or painted over by Picasso himself, but one work which we would definitely assert was done there — done, perhaps, in the Pallarès house, on a sketch from life — is that *Procession* of women towards a hermitage which is evidently that of Sant Salvador, dated in *The Picassos of Picasso* 1895/96, and which we must place, therefore, in the period of 1898/99.

Picasso returned to Barcelona alone in February 1899. He had completely recovered his health, he had even worked a little and, above all, he was returning with the strength of a bull, ready for battle.

24. The studio at No. 2 in "Calle de Escudellers Blancs". The return from Horta marks the beginning of Picasso's really bohemian life in Barcelona. His refusal to live under his parents' roof, although he had been reconciled with his family, forced him to share studios, and sometimes lodgings, with other painters, nearly always better off than he.

During his absence there had been some changes: though the nightmare of the Cuban war had ended, social agitation, on the other hand, was increasing. The "4

58. Jaume Sabartés as a "decadent poet". Barcelona, 1900. Charcoal and water-colour on paper, 48 × 32 cm. Picasso Museum, Barcelona.

59. Jaume Sabartés. Barcelona, 1900. Charcoal and water-colour on paper, 50.5 × 33 cm. Picasso Museum, Barcelona.

60. Ricard Opisso. Barcelona, 1900. Drawing with coloured background, 31 × 22 cm. J. A. Samaranch Collection, Barcelona.

61. Joaquim Mir. Barcelona, 1899. Coloured drawing.
62. Pujolà i Vallés. Barcelona, 1899. Coloured drawing.
63. Carles Casagemas. Barcelona, 1899. Coloured drawing.
64. Santiago Rusiñol. Barcelona, 1899. Coloured drawing.
65. Picasso (self-portrait). Barcelona, 1899. Coloured drawing.
66. Pere Romeu. Barcelona, 1899. Coloured drawing.
67. Juli Vallmitjana. Barcelona, 1899. Coloured drawing.
68. Ramon Pitxot. Barcelona, 1899. Coloured drawing.
69. Soler. Barcelona, 1899. Coloured drawing.
70. Ramon Casas. Barcelona, 1899. Coloured drawing.
71. H. Anglada Camarasa. Barcelona, 1899. Coloured drawing.
72. Manolo Hugué. Barcelona, 1900.
73. Joan Gay. Barcelona, 1900.
74. H. Anglada Camarasa. Barcelona, 1900.
75. The composer Morera. Barcelona, 1900. Charcoal drawing, 18 × 13 cm. Jordi Gimferrer Collection, Banyoles (Gerona).
76. Ramon Pitxot. Barcelona, 1900.
77. Josep M. Folch i Torres. Barcelona, 1900.
78. J. Vallhonrat. Barcelona, 1900.
79. J. Vidal Ventosa, Barcelona, 1900. Charcoal drawing with brown-coloured background. According to Vidal Ventosa, this background was obtained by dipping the brush into a cup containing coffee grounds mixed with water. 47 × 27,5 cm. Picasso Museum, Barcelona.

80. Cinto Reventós. Barcelona, 1900. Charcoal drawing, 42 × 34 cm. Dr Cinto Reventós Collection, Barcelona.
81. The tailor Soler. Barcelona, 1900.

61

62

63

64

69

70

71

77

78

79

80

82. Angel F. de Soto (unpublished).
83. Josep Rocarol. Barcelona, 1900.

84. Mateu F. de Soto. Barcelona, 1900.
85. Joan B. Fonte. Barcelona, 1900. Charcoal drawing, 52 × 32.7 cm. Fogg Art Museum, Harvard University, Cambridge, Massachusetts.

65

66

67

68

72

73

74

75

76

82

83

84

85

86. Angel F. de Soto. Barcelona, 1900. Charcoal drawing, 43 × 24 cm. Autograph of Picasso, on the back of a photograph of the drawing, recognizing it as his own work.
87. Drawing done by Picasso in 1898, which appeared in the Almanac of the "Esquella de la Torratxa" for the year 1899.

Gats" had achieved a certain prestige, and Xavier Gosé, Nonell, Regoyos and Pitxot had all exhibited there. Pere Romeu had published a review with the name of his establishment, the *"4 Gats"*, but just at this time it disappeared, giving place before long (June 3rd) to another review, which was to be of great importance in the artistic life of the city: "Pèl & Ploma", with illustrations by Ramon Casas and edited by Miquel Utrillo. This year also saw the fourth centenary of the birth of Velázquez.

At first Picasso shared a studio with the brother of the sculptor Cardona. It has always been thought that this studio was at No. 1 in the Calle de Escudellers Blancs, but in my book *Picasso i els seus amics catalans* I have already pointed out that it must really have been No. 2, for both the sculptor Josep Cardona and his brother Santiago, who was a painter, showed at the 1896 Fine Arts Exhibition, and both have their address as No. 2, Calle de Escudellers Blancs.

Sabartés, who first met Picasso in this flat, where he had been taken by Mateo F. de Soto, told me that Picasso occupied a tiny room in the flat, the rest of which was a corset-maker's workshop. With this information in mind I can now give another detail, hitherto unpublished, which further confirms my hypothesis: an advertisement for "La Imperial" corsets which appeared regularly for quite a long time in the pages of "La Vanguardia", and

Poem by J. Oliva Bridgman, accompanied by a photograph which inspired Picasso's illustration for *The virgins' clamour* by the same author (unpublished document).

88. Illustration for *To be or not to be*, by J. Oliva Bridgman, published in the magazine "Joventut" on 16th August 1900. Barcelona.

89. Illustration for *The virgins' clamour*, by J. Oliva Bridgman, published in the magazine "Joventut" on 12th July 1900. Barcelona.

89

Christiansen.

ODA A FRINE

Friné, filla de Tespia: la distancia
de sigles y més sigles que'ns allunya,
ab rápit vol mon esperit la esborra.
Et sento,'t tinch aprop; ma fantasía
et veu com Praxitel·les: bella estatua
cisellada per Venus afrodita
y á son imatje feta. Y res detura
el cant que ix de mon cor al contemplarte;
que ha sacudit mos nirvis ta bellesa,
y ha encés mas sanchs la teva carn nevada,
y han despertat tots mos anhels; y, alegre,
porto la copa dels grans plers als llabis.

Superba joya de la edat antiga:
jo, com el poble de la invicta Atenas,
eixir te miro de las onas blavas,
nda't contemplo embadalit, y uneixo
ma veu als cántichs d'aquell poble il·lustre.
Salve, Friné, filla de Tespia! Salve!

Nús't contemplo enfront dels jutjes; roja
sa testa calva veig tornarse al véurer;
els veig, inútils, á tos peus rendirse,
y't veig burlante de sos prechs estúpits!...

Y á Venus veig, que's sent apesarada
contemplant ta hermosor, que's sent gelosa
de tas carns sugestivas... Que sufreixi!

No escoltis sos gemechs, Friné, no escoltis
la veu del que pateix. Gosém la vida,
la vida del plaher!

Soch teu y ets meva:
la Joventut me fa senyor; la Forma
me fa esclàu teu, Friné: soch rey, sent súbdit.
Ja sé qu'haig de trobar entre tos brassos
la Mort: mes no m'espanta, si es hermosa.
Vinga la Mort, vinga eixa Mort temuda,
y ensemps que clogui mos febrosos llabis,
las flors marceixi que mon front coronin;
las flors de nostra festa. Quan, gastada
pels plers la carn del cos, no tinga forsa
y com bambolla de sabó's desfassi,
vinga la Mort ab tos petons unida,
y ab mon ultim esfors voli mon ánima!

Gosém, Friné, gosém! La vida es curta
quan es ditxosa com la nostra; eterna
quan es teixit de sufriments! Tos llabis
guardan el néctar del plaher: gosemlo!
Abrassam fort contra ton pit, apretam
contra aqueix pit hont niuha la luxuria;
abrassam fort contra tas carns rosadas;
contra ta forma esculptural ofegam!

Fidel no m'ho serás: m'ho diu ta historia;
mes tant se val: ets franca y t'ho perdono.
Tu no m'enganyas ab els ulls hipócritas
d'aquella verge qu'ofereix la ditxa
reflectintla en la pau de sas miradas;
tu no pots enganyarme: de tos llabis
no surten juraments d'amor fermíssim,
que s'esfuman ensemps que las paraulas.
Ets meva quan te tinch entre mos brassos;
mes ta pensa es molt lluny: á mas caricias
respón el cos, no l'ánima. La teva
somnia ab un altre home, que al besarte
caurá com jo cauré: dins l'ampla fossa
qu'obra á tos peus l'enervador cansanci.
Ja ho sé, Friné; mes no per 'xó m'espanto,
ni t'insulto per 'xó. Tu no mentéixes;
com has sigut ets ara y serás sempre:
la eterna variació! Tu ets la enemiga
del vici que s'amaga entre las ombras
d'una virtut hipócrita: ton vici
es gran com ta bellesa sobirana
y ayma la llum del sol com las flors l'ayman!

Gosém, Friné, gosém! Avuy encara
despertan á un sol bes nostres desitjos.
Demá... ¿qui ho sab? Potser demá't cansanci
ens allunyi per sempre! Friné hermosa:
superba joya de la edat antiga:
no hi pensém en demá; vinga com vulla!
¿El present es hermós? Gosemlo alegres!
¿El pervindre es fatal? No hi pensém ara!
La vida es el moment que's viu; la vida
es un soch, no un seré! Friné tespiana:
cantém els plers de nostre amor, y'ls homes
viscan com han viscut y viurán sempre,
eternament burlantse dels que gosan!

JOAN OLIVA BRIDGMAN.

90. Illustration for the short story *The madwoman*, by Surinyac Senties, published in the review "Catalunya Artística" on 6th September 1900. Barcelona.

90

which gave the trade address as No. 2, Calle de Escudellers Blancs.

At the "4 Gats", which from then on was one of his most usual haunts, and where he often stayed to dine, he made new acquaintances and friends: Nonell, Sebastià Junyent, Manolo, Ors, Ramon Pitxot, Casagemas, Vidal Ventosa...

Sebastià Junyer-Vidal had just had an exhibition in the "Sala Parés"; he had fallen in love with the island of Majorca, and he had already made his first trip to Paris. Ramon Pitxot had just built himself a house in Cadaqués and was preparing an exhibition for Paris of pictures painted in and around village.

This was the moment when Catalonia, through her renaissance, discovered her own physical body; when the painters, like true lovers, felt an urge to depict the forms of their country, each one seeking some place hitherto unexplored and in accord with his temperament. The vogue of Impressionism, which drove the artists out of their studios to work in the open air, was a contributory factor in affirming this tendency.

At that time there were frequent riots in the University, and the students of the "Lonja" either took part in these or even

91. Carles Casagemas, full-face and in profile. Barcelona, 1900. Drawing, 13 ×
 21 cm. J. A. Samaranch Collection, Barcelona.
92. Fita y Fita, Picasso's pupil. Barcelona, 1900.
93. Antoni Busquets i Punset, a prizewinner at the Floral Games. Drawing
 published in the review "Catalunya Artística" on 6 th September 1900. Lead
 pencil and charcoal on paper, 17.5 × 12.7 cm. Private collection, Barcelona.

92

93

94. Bullfight. 1900. Oil on canvas, 47 × 56 cm. Galerie Georges Petit, Paris.

95. Bullfight. Barcelona, 1901. Charcoal and pastel, 15×22 cm. Private
collection, Barcelona (unpublished).

96. Bullfight. 1900. Gouache, 16.2×30.5 cm. Cau Ferrat Museum, Sitges (Barcelona).

96

took precedence in the outbreaks. Jaume Sabartés, in his work *From the "Lonja" to the Picasso Museum,* says: "Many of us students of the 'Lonja' were not only Catalans but Catalanists, and the festival of the Floral Games was a splendid excuse for us to exalt our youthful sentiments or, to put it more clearly, our 'anti-every-thing' zeal, our rebellion against what we considered official, because we were young, and it was Spring. At the end of the poetic 'jousts' we sang *'Els Segadors'* (The Reapers), the Catalan war song, which was forbidden. (...) Picasso did not take long to understand and speak Cata-lan — or to sing *'Els Segadors'* either, attracted as he was by the very efferves-cence of Catalanism."

97. Bullfight. 1901. Oil on canvas, 53 × 68 cm. Niarchos Collection.

On Sunday afternoons they often forgathered in a flat that belonged to Casagemas above the arcade known as the "Arc de Cirés", where they held literary contests. They had a big bowl there for making punch, which they drank through straws. Apparently these meetings were also attended by the Reventós brothers, the Soto brothers and Vidal Ventosa. It

was were, too, at that time of experiments and novelties of all sorts, that they "fried" their drawings, exactly as if they were frying eggs. Casagemas had many of these, and Picasso himself fried more than one.

From time to time they went on from this flat to spend the evening at the house of Vidal Ventosa, who had a ground-floor

An article by Pere de Roda (Wenceslao F. de Soto) which appeared in "La Noche" on 12th October 1927, recalling Picasso's friends of the "4 Gats" period and accompanied by some unpublished portraits of them (unpublished document).

flat in the Plaza del Pino, where they used to take chairs outside in summer to enjoy the cool evening air. Evidently, Picasso's participation in the disturbances at the Lonja did not exactly please his father, who was still making his laborious ascent by seniority on the roster of professors, year after year until he finally reached the first rank.

Whether there was some clash between them on this account, or whether the youthful Picasso's impetuous temperament brought him to such a pass, it is certain that he spent several weeks at about this time in a house of ill fame, where he decorated completely the walls of the room where they harboured him. It is from that year, and surely from those turbulent weeks, that we must date the *Barcelona nocturne*, in which he describes the desolating spectacle of that wretched existence. Some of the drawings reveal its intimate, picturesque details. But the force of Picasso is so great that in a few moments we forget the subjects and are carried away by his sublime drawing.

25. 1900. The year 1900 was one of redoubled ebullition and restlessness for all the young spirits of the time. Some of

98. Pere Manyac, Picasso's first dealer. Paris, 1901. Oil on canvas, 100.5 × 67.5 cm. National Gallery of Art (Chester Dale Collection), Washington, D. C.
99. Jaume Sabartés, one of the last works painted by Picasso in Paris in 1901 or early in 1902. Oil on canvas, 46 × 38 cm. Picasso Museum, Barcelona.

the papers, like "La Vanguardia", echoed the argument that was going on all over Europe, as to whether the twentieth century began that year or the next. But as life is stronger than theories, certain decisive factors settled the question in favour of the former thesis, especially the Universal Exhibition in Paris. This city already attracted artists, on account of the avant-garde currents which flowed from it, but the Exhibition provided an irresistible incentive for going.

In 1900 Picasso was eighteen years old.

In its thirtieth issue, which came out on 23rd December 1899, the review "Pèl & Ploma" had announced a competition for posters advertising the 1900 Carnival. Entries were to be deposited at the "4 Gats".

Picasso entered for this competition, but did not win the prize. It would be interesting today, after so many years, to see the prize-winning poster and discover the basis for the committee's decision.

At all events, in the thirty-second issue of "Pèl & Ploma", which was published on 6th January 1900, the result was duly announced:

"At the '4 Gats' may be seen the Carnival posters, easily the best of which is the one by Roig. Undoubtedly, too, the next best is that done by Picazo (sic), if we are to judge the works on the basis of originality and good technique. And thus it has been decided by the worthy members of the committee, Mir, Hugué (Manolo) and Planellas."

I have no doubt at all that the poster, or the sketches for the poster, can be traced in those drawings in which we see a shouting pierrot with his arm round the waist of a woman on his left.

26. No. 17, "Riera de Sant Joan". As if to mark the entry of the new century with a certain solemnity, at the beginning of the year Picasso, along with Carles Casagemas, moved into the studio at No. 17 in the street known as "Riera de Sant Joan" (literally: St. John's Stream). Sabartés is definite on this point: according to him, Picasso remained here from the beginning of the year until the following September.

The walls of this studio-flat were immediately decorated by Picasso and Casagemas, thus providing them, pictorially at least, with all the conveniences the two artists lacked: a wardrobe with a looking-glass, a safe, a larder, and even a manservant and a generously proportioned maid,

PETRVS
MANACH-

Picasso

100. Pen-and-ink drawing, accompanying a poem by P. Prat Jabal·lí published by the review "Auba" in its April 1902 number (unpublished document).

101. The "4 Gats" circle, with Picasso in the foreground, Pere Romeu on his left and, behind him, Rocarol, Fontbona, Angel F. de Soto and Jaume Sabartés, standing. Barcelona, 1902. Pen and ink, 31 × 34 cm.

a) The Plaza de l'Oli, first home of the "Guayaba" (top-floor flat on the right).

b) The flat roofs above the studio in the Calle Nueva (now the Calle Conde del Asalto), Barcelona.

100

AVBA

— Picasso —

Apunte, per Pau R. Picasso

HIMNE DE PRIMAVERA

Les pulcres neus de l' hivernada,
S' han fós als raigs benignes del nou sol,
I un somrís de bonança benhaurada,
Ha devallat del cel am tendre vol.

S' han fós les neus al bes de nova vida.
Els cels han devingut blaus i serens,
I la terra com mare amorosida,
Ha fet neixe en son cor nova florida,
Qu' ha omplert el mon de cántics i d' encens.

Les aus han enlairat noves complantes,
Tot fent llurs nius d' amor;
En els jardins s' han adreçat les plantes,
De fulles verdejantes;
Les ponzelles flairoses i arrogantes,
S' han badat al copsar tanta claror.

Els rierols, anguilejant pels boscos,
S' han desfét am sospirs,
I s' han perdut despres am sorolls foscos,
Com l' aleteig dolcíssim dels zefirs.
Se mou la sava tota xardorosa
I les flors se feconden pels jardins.....
Cantem, com canten am veu harmoniosa,
Les flors al revrer els sospirs divins.

PERE PRAT JABAL-LI

101

awaiting the orders of the two tenants. It was in this studio, also as if to mark the entry of the new century, that Picasso and Casagemas prepared their first exhibition and their first trip to Paris.

27. Exhibition in the "4 Gats". Almost all Picasso's biographers place this exhibition in 1897 or 1898. Various reasons made us suspect that it must have been later, and today we can give, undoubtedly for the first time, the necessary proof. The exhibition certainly opened on February 1st, 1900. The evening edition of "La Veu de Catalunya" that day seems to prove it: An exhibition of drawings and paintings

102. Card announcing the birth of Pere and Corina Romeu's son. Barcelona, 12th May 1902. Postcard, 9 × 14 cm. Private collection, Barcelona.

103. Postcard advertising "Lecitina Agell". Barcelona, 1902. Postcard, 9 × 14 cm. J. Palau i Fabre Collection, Barcelona.

104. The dead woman. Barcelona, 1902-1903. Oil on canvas, 44.5 × 34.1 cm. Picasso-Reventós Foundation, Barcelona.

105. Portrait of S. Junyer-Vidal by Picasso, reproduced in "El Liberal" on 16th October 1902, on the occasion of an exhibition by the former (unpublished document).

b

102

Na Corina y En Pere Romeu
(Hostalers dels Quatre Gats)
es complauen en ferli á saber
el naixement del primer fill
(12 Maig 1902)
Pere Romeu
Jáuregui
Padrí: Esteve Huguet
Padrina: Josefa Malgá

103

La Lecitina Agell

Cura siempre el linfatismo
y la debilidad ósea

105

SALÓN PARÉS
EXPOSICION JUÑER-VIDAL

by R. Picasso has opened in the gallery of the "4 Gats". And in "La Vanguardia" of February 3rd there was a review which, for its own interest and because it is the first review of the first exhibition by the first artist of our time, we quote here in its entirety.

"The *IV Gats*. Exhibition by Ruiz Picazzo (sic). — A young man, hardly more than a child, Ruiz Picazzo, has opened an exhibition of drawings and colour sketches in the *4 Gats*.

"In all the works exhibited he shows extraordinary facility in the use of brush and pencil, and so their principal characteristic is the elegance of the drawing, a factor which is always welcome, but becomes prejudicial when it is given precedence over every other quality and is not the result of long and conscientious practice.

"Hence the lack of balance to be noted in the drawings and canvasses of Picazzo. At first glance they may cause a good impression — however one sees immediately that the painter is more often than not influenced by alien tendencies. On the other hand, when we come to analyse them, we can see signs of inexperience and carelessness, perfectly excusable consider-ing the age of the painter, and above all a certain hesitation as to the course it would be best for him to follow.

"It is not, of course, easy for a young artist to find his bearings; the élite who are able to channel their possibilities from the beginning are few indeed; but it is no less certain that, to achieve a personal style in art, one must not seek it in that of other painters and simply follow blindly in their tracks; on the contrary, one should follow other paths and beware of picking up the crumbs of the masters, that easy bait which leads to the perdition of most young artists.

"This reflexion is suggested by the series of charcoal portraits drawn by the young artist in question, portraits which are undoubtedly spoiled by their back-grounds, where the painter shows most evidently the lack of experience to which we have referred above.

"We must admit, however, that many of these portraits have *character*, which is important, and that some of them are sketched with a pleasing sobriety, worthy of mention in all of them being, as we have said, the ease in the use of the pencil, a predominant feature of the rest of the drawings and sketches shown.

106. The blue houses. Barcelona, 1902. Oil, 50.5 × 40.5 cm.
107. Front page of the daily newspaper "El Liberal" on 5th October 1902, evoking the traditional Barcelona festivities of Our Lady of Ransom. Barcelona.

84

108. Drunk woman drowsing (or "The absinthe drinker"). Barcelona, 1902. Oil on
canvas, 80 × 62 cm. Dr Huber Collection, Glarus (Switzerland).

109. Woman squatting. Barcelona, 1902. Oil on canvas, 63.5 × 50 cm. Carl Bertel
     Collection, Nathorst, Stockholm.

109

110. Seated woman. Picasso's first sculpture. Barcelona, 1902. Replica in bronze, 15 × 11.5 × 8.5 cm. Picasso Museum, Barcelona.

111. The woman with a chignon. Barcelona, 1902. Oil on canvas, 100 × 69 cm. Formerly in the Paul Guillaume Collection, Paris.

110

111

112. Nude from behind. Barcelona, 1902. Oil on canvas, 46×40 cm. Private
collection, Paris.

112

113. The woman with the shawl. Barcelona, 1902. Oil on canvas, 65 × 54 cm.
     Galerie Georges Petit, Paris.
114. Mother and children on the seashore. Barcelona, 1903. Pastel, 46 × 31 cm.

114

113

115. Portrait of Corina Jáuregui, Pere Romeu's wife. Barcelona, 1902. Oil on canvas, 60×48 cm. Formerly in the Picasso Collection.

115

116. Cocottes in the bar. Barcelona, 1902. Oil on canvas, 80 × 91.5 cm. M. Walter P. Chrysler Jr Collection, New York.

117. Poor people on the seashore, Barcelona, 1903. Oil on wooden panel, 105.4 × 69 cm. Chester Dale Collection, National Gallery of Art, Washington.

16 117

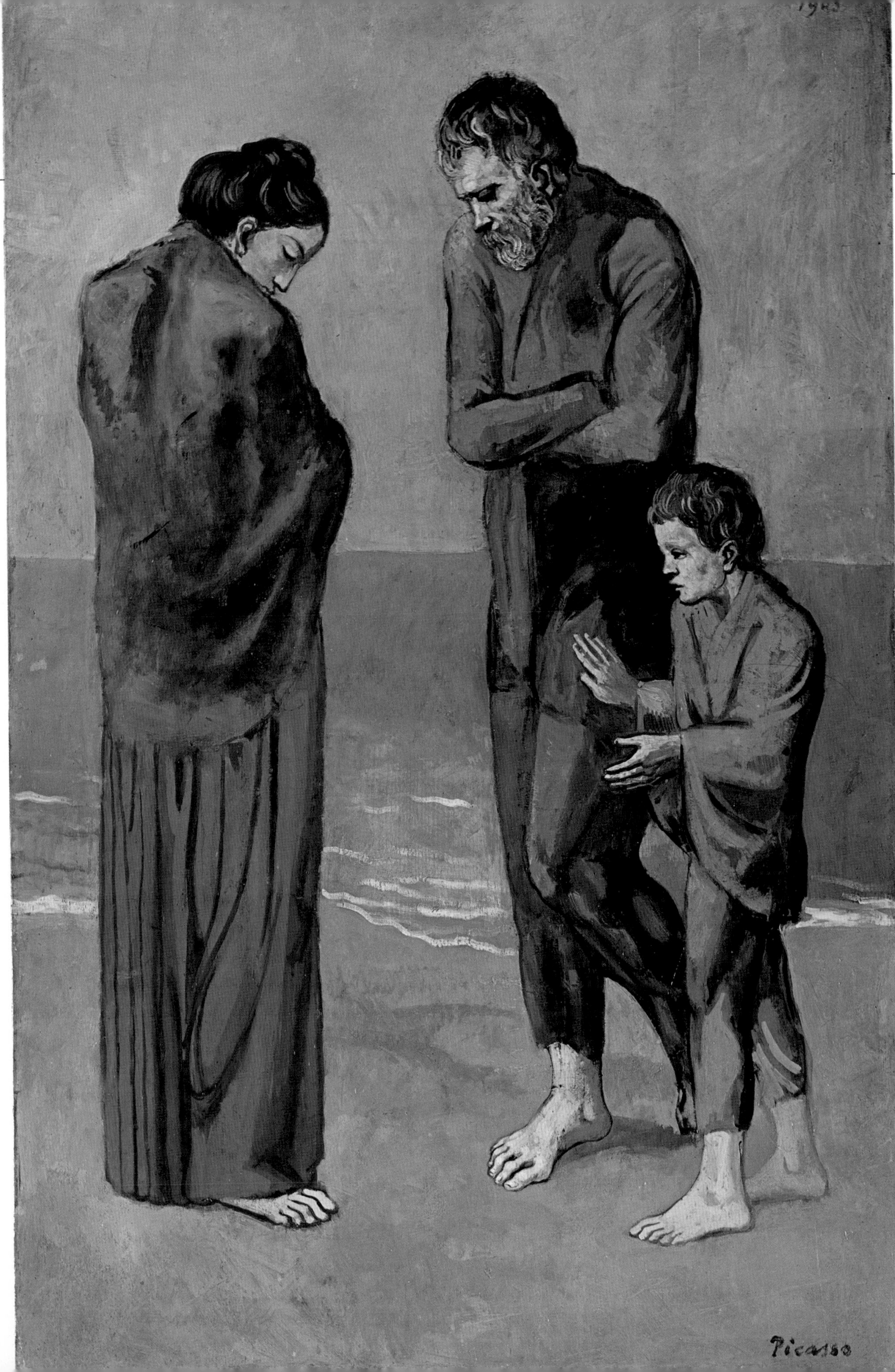

118. The housetops of Barcelona. Barcelona, 1903. Oil on canvas, 71 × 112 cm. Formerly in the Picasso Collection.

119. Barcelona nocturne, from the studio in the Riera de Sant Joan. Barcelona, 1903, 54 × 45.5 cm. E. G. Bührle Family Collection, Zürich.

118

"The only painting shown by Ruiz Picazzo in the "4 Gats" represents a young priest, standing with a prayer book in his hand and looking at a dying woman. An oil lamp sheds a faint light, reflected at intervals on the white counterpane of the woman's bed. The rest of the picture is in shadow, which tones down still further the indefinite silhouettes of the figures.

"In this work, painted with considerable naturalness, there are some features not to be despised; characteristics which may be expected to mature when Sr. Ruiz Picazzo, without prejudices of any kind and with a greater store of experience and study than hitherto, reaches an age at which artists strive to achieve everything possible and to paint really personal works."

Interminable commentaries could be made on the above, so we shall not make any. Suffice it to say that the article, attributed to Rodríguez Codolá, a professor of the "Lonja" and critic of "La Vanguardia", is not signed. From the tone and the reflections of the writer, one can see, above all, the gentle scolding of a teacher, perhaps a friendly admonition given on behalf of his colleague, the painter's father.

The principal anomaly, however, is in the fact that the article was not written by Alfredo Opisso, the paper's official art critic, who reviewed all the exhibitions in Barcelona, however insignificant. This makes it difficult not to think that there may have been a certain animosity in the air against Picasso. But why? Because he was not Catalan? But the younger generation already crowded around Picasso, whom they considered an outstandingly gifted leader of the avant-garde.

This exhibition, as may be guessed from the review in "La Vanguardia", consisted of a great number of drawings on very different subjects, though with a marked preponderance of portraits of Picasso's friends and colleagues, done in pencil, charcoal and ink-wash. It was these portraits that formed that gallery of Barcelona characters, among whom there were some who were already famous, like Rusiñol and Mir, and a great number as yet unknown: Sabartés, Rocarol, Cinto and Ramon Reventós, Vidal Ventosa, Angel and Mateo F. de Soto, Riera, Cardona, etc.

As for sales, it would appear that some collectors bought a few drawings. Most of the sales, however, were made at bargain prices — a peseta or two each — and even these can hardly have been numerous, for many years later quite a lot of these drawings were still in Picasso's possession.

28. Picasso in Sitges and Badalona. Before leaving for Paris, but almost certainly after their respective exhibitions at the "4 Gats", Casagemas persuaded Picasso to accompany him to spend a day in Sitges. This little town, thanks to the Modernista movement and the recent unveiling of the monument to El Greco, had become quite an important place in the Catalan art world. The Casagemas family had a house there.

Another day Casagemas' fancy took the two friends to Badalona, where he also had a small estate, called Cal General. In Badalona they visited the cemetery and afterwards Picasso posed for Casagemas, who did a "stillborn portrait" of his friend — that is to say he drew nothing at all, as though boasting of his congenital nihilism.

29. First illustrations. On February 24th, "La Vanguardia" published the final list of the Barcelona artists who were competing in the official contest for the honour of exhibiting in the Paris Exhi-

bition, and among them we find the name of Picasso, though he calls himself simply Pablo Ruiz, who presented oil paintings.

We also know that at this time Picasso, surely much against his will as a creative artist, gave some private drawing lessons. We have a witness to this in the form of the portrait of one of his pupils, Fita y Fita, drawn by Picasso himself.

Picasso's activities were manifold and grew with the century. That year he was commissioned to illustrate several texts in various publications of the period. He had already published, as has been pointed out, a drawing in the almanac of "L'Esquella de la Torratxa" for the year 1899 (this almanac was usually published at the beginning of December of the preceding year). But that drawing was not an illustration properly speaking, nor did it easily lend itself to reproduction. Perhaps that was why Utrillo overlooked it when he wrote, in 1901, that the glory of first place belonged to the Catalanist magazine "Joventut", which in its twenty-second number, on 12th July 1900 (page 345), published a drawing by Picasso accompanying a poem by Joan Oliva Bridgman entitled *El clam de les verges* (The virgins' clamour). And the twenty-seventh num-

120. The offering. 1902. Drawing in India ink, 25 × 26 cm. Mr and Mrs Sidney Elliot Cahn Collection, New York. .

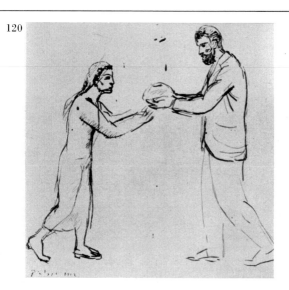

120

ber of the same magazine, which came out on 16th August of the same year (page 424), carried another drawing of Picasso's, accompanying another poem by the same author, with the Shakespearean title *To be or not to be*.

The following month the review "Catalunya Artística" published, in its thirteenth number, on 6th September (page 208), a portrait of the poet Anton Busquets i Punset, who had won a prize at the Floral Games; and in its seventeenth number, on 4th October (page 268), an illustration to a story by Surinyac Senties called *The madwoman*.

The first of these illustrations, *El clam de les verges*, was a fairly literal adaptation of a photograph that had appeared in the eleventh number of the same magazine, "Joventut", accompanying an *Ode to Friné* by Oliva Bridgman. The girl in the photograph, whose name is given as Cristensen, must have been Oliva Bridgman's ideal of feminine beauty. For those who knew Picasso it is not difficult to guess what probably happened: Oliva Bridgman must have praised this Cristensen so extravagantly that Picasso, in his desire to please him (that inner desire, so typical of Picasso, to adapt his work to

please everybody!), drew the same girl for his friend.

The review "Pèl & Ploma" was now also published in Castilian, and though its contents were basically the same as in the Catalan edition, there were still some minor differences. Thus, for instance, in the number that appeared in Castilian on 15th September there was a portrait of the poet Eduardo Marquina by Picasso which did not appear in the Catalan edition.

All these illustrations, as has been pointed out, were done with the same technique and in the same spirit; they echo the Wagnerianism and Nordic influence then prevailing in Barcelona. But in Picasso's work these influences are lessened and the spirit of an innate classicism shows through.

121. The soup. Barcelona, 1902 or 1903. Oil on canvas, 37 × 45 cm. J. H. Crang
Collection, Toronto, Canada.

It should be noted that these four illustrations were published in four successive months (July, August, September and October of 1900), which would appear to indicate that Picasso had finally entered into the life of Barcelona and was accepted in its artistic circles. Four more months were to elapse, however, before he had another drawing published. Sabartés, moreover, tells us that certain magazines of the period absolutely refused Picasso's work and that some of them — "L'Esquella de la Torratxa" and "La Campana de Gràcia", for instance — did not even return his drawings.

Albert Maluquer has recorded that among the thousands of drawings he acquired when he bought up the stock of "L'Esquella de la Torratxa" he found an envelope containing a portrait of Picasso and two of the artist's drawings, accompanied by a letter from Blanco Coris recommending them for publication. On the outside of the envelope were the words "Too bad to be published".

This, as we may see for ourselves, is but a relative truth, considering the drawing that had appeared a year before in the same magazine's almanac. If it is true that one of the drawings found by Albert Maluquer was the one that showed that girl with a bucket at her feet, I must say that the opinion the editors of "L'Esquella de la Torratxa" had of Picasso's drawings was a very mistaken one, for the drawing in question is not only of excellent quality but is also much more suitable for reproduction, since it is a pen-and-ink drawing with very clean, assured lines.

30. Passing through Barcelona. We already know that in the autumn of the year 1900 Picasso and Casagemas made their first trip to Paris and that they both returned to Barcelona around Christmas, though they only stayed for a few days, for the New Year found them in Malaga, Casagemas later returning to Barcelona and Paris, while Picasso, as he had done in 1897, went to Madrid.

31. "Young Art". In Madrid he joined forces with a Catalan, Francesc de A. Soler, to bring out a new review which largely reflected recent events in Barcelona. This time he had not come to Madrid to copy the old masters in the Prado, but to introduce a new art; hence the title of *"Arte Joven"* (Young Art). The review had to cease publication after four issues,

122. The unkempt girl. Barcelona, 1903. Water-colour on paper, 50 × 37 cm. (In this picture, as in others of the same period, the colouring material used may have been a sort of Reckitt's blue, a cheap product which Picasso used and mixed with other materials in preparing his colours.) Picasso Museum, Barcelona.

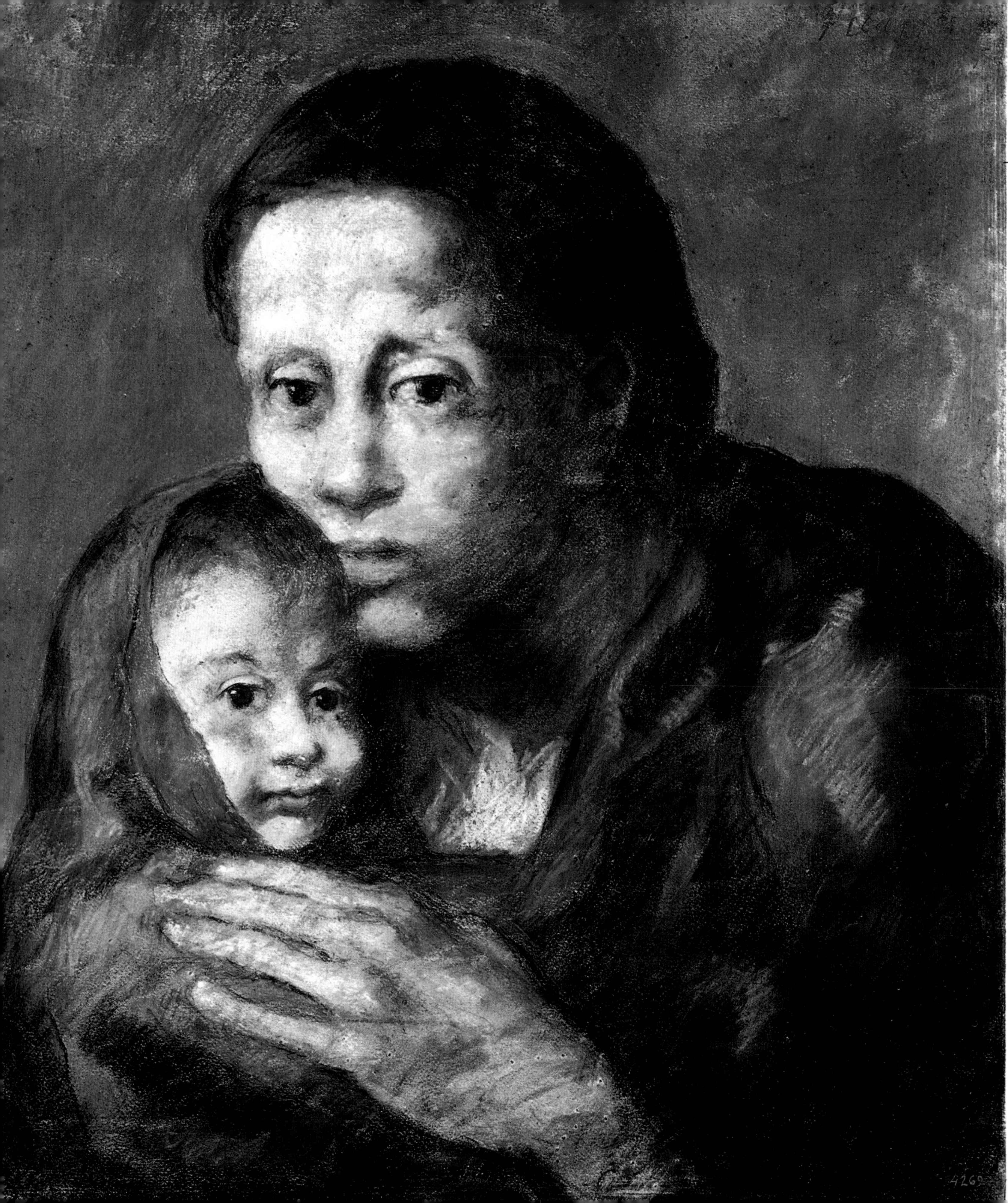

123. "Forsaken". Barcelona, 1903. Pastel and charcoal on paper, 46×40 cm. Picasso Museum, Barcelona.

though not before announcing another publication, *"Madrid, notas de Arte"* (Madrid, Art Notes), which, however, never saw the light. Picasso returned to Barcelona about the middle of May, 1901.

32. Exhibition at the "Sala Parés". Thanks to the sagacity of Miquel Utrillo, who doubtless wished to keep Picasso in Catalonia, the magazine "Pèl & Ploma" organized an exhibition of works by Ramon Casas and pastels by Picasso at the "Sala Parés" — *the Barcelona gallery par excellence* —, and included, in its June number of 1901 (which came out late), a most flattering article by Miquel Utrillo himself (signed Pincell), accompanied by reproductions of five works by Picasso and a portrait of him by Ramon Casas.

Among other observations, Miquel Utrillo declared: "Picasso's art is tremendously young; born of a spirit of observation which hàs no pity for the weakneses of his contemporaries, we can see in it even the beauties of what is hideous, noted with the sobriety of an artist who draws because he sees, not because he knows how to draw noses from memory."

From the Barcelona point of view, the honour could scarcely have been greater. All this must have occurred during the month of June, but Picasso probably neither attended the opening of his exhibition nor was able to wait for the number of "Pèl & Ploma" that reviewed it so favourably. When it came out he was already back in Paris with Jaume Andreu.

His sudden departure for Paris seems to have been mainly due to the insistence of Manyac, his first dealer, who was pressing him for the works he had been promised. On 24th June that year an exhibition of 75 pictures by Picasso opened at the Galerie Vollard in Paris.

Picasso returned to Barcelona at the beginning of January 1902, having already begun, in Paris, his Blue Period.

33. "Guayaba". During the month of January 1902, Joan Vidal Ventosa and Quim Borralleres set up house together in a studio at No. 4 in the Plaça de l'Oli.

It was an artist's model who christened the new studio "Guayaba", a corruption of Valhalla, the resting-place to which the Valkyries brought the spirits of warriors slain on the field, and this name gives us fresh evidence of the great influence of Wagnerianism in Barcelona.

This studio, where Vidal Ventosa produced pyrogravures and which Pere Inglada was later to use for drawing, eventually became one of the most popular meeting-places for artists of its day. Apart from those already mentioned, it was a favourite haunt of Salvador Ventosa, Cinto Reventós (soon to become one of the most eminent doctors in Barcelona), Ramon Reventós, the short-story writer, Salvador Teyà, Pere Luandre, Enric Jardí, Eugeni d'Ors, Diego Ruiz, Isidre Nonell, Francesc Labarta, J. M. Junoy, Feliu Elies, Manolo Hugué, Smith, the Soto brothers, etc. — and, of course, Picasso.

In the artistic life of Barcelona, 1902 was also a year dominated by the reputation and personality of Nonell.

34. The Calle Conde del Asalto. Back in Barcelona, Picasso returned to the house of his parents, with whom he had been completely reconciled, but in order to safeguard his independence he soon took a new studio in the Calle Nueva (now called the Calle Conde del Asalto), almost next door to the *café chantant* "Edèn Concert", where he once more formed the habit of going to sketch the girls.

This studio had been rented by the painter Rocarol, but Angel F. de Soto occupied part of it and paid half the rent.

The Blue Period continued to develop here but, according to what Jaume Sabartés told me, the blue tones were new stronger, in accord with the light of Barcelona and much more intense, which is why they came to be known, years later, as *the blues of Barcelona*. When Sabartés returned from Paris in the spring of 1902, he at once went to visit Picasso at this studio, and one of the things he was shown was a Barcelona townscape representing the neighbouring housetops.

Picasso, that imaginative creator of so many scenes, situations, characters and fables, was such a great painter that he could easily confine himself, when it suited him, to pure, naked reality — even to the absolutely prosaic if necessary.

Surely from this period, too, is an advertisement for a pharmaceutical product — "Lecitina Agell" — with a drawing that showed a pierrot and his girl, the former with his finger pointing at the name of the product. The model for the male figure, with his sinewy neck, seems to be the one we see in several paintings of this period, done some months before in Paris, like *The two tumblers*, now in the Moscow Museum, or the *Harlequin* with his elbows resting on the table and two fingers on his cheek, which is in the Museum of Modern Art in New York.

By now an accepted regular at the "4 Gats", he designed the announcement of the birth of a son to Pere and Corina Romeu on 12th May 1902, as well as doing several drawings of the establishment, one of them in almost Gothic colouring, rather in the manner of Hassal. He also did some pencil or pen-and-ink sketches of his fellow habitués, in which he used the same signature as he had for the "Lecitina Agell" advertisement: a P within a circle.

But all this work, even when paid for, cannot have brought in very much, for Sabartés years later remembered how Picasso, when alone in the "4 Gats" in the evenings, would frequently play the slot-machines of those days and, thanks to patient and complex calculations, would manage to make a few centimos from them every day.

This Bohemian life contrasted sharply with his elegant clothes, his cane and other accoutrements. The fact is that Picasso, like other artists of the period, had made the acquaintance of the tailor Soler (alias "Retalls"), with his shop in the Portal de l'Angel, who was willing to dress him in exchange for a few drawings — and a little later on, as we shall see, for some paintings. From time to time Picasso even stayed to lunch or dinner with Soler and his wife.

On some occasions, too, especially with the Reventós brothers, he used to go and eat mussels and drink wine from a *porrón* (a carafe from which one drinks through a tapering side-spout) at "La Musclera" (The Mussel-house), or he would spend the evening at the "Cinematógrafo Napoleón", which was the great novelty of the day in Barcelona.

At times, too, he had dinner at the house of the Junyer-Vidal brothers, the owners of a cotton warehouse, who had offices at No. 21 in the Calle de la Platería. There he would spend long hours in a back room of the offices, drawing almost all the time — and these drawings were carefully kept by the Junyer-Vidal brothers, who finally amassed quite a collection.

Picasso's signature had gradually developed, during these years, from the original formula of Pablo Picasso to the simple name Picasso, passing through such intermediate stages as Pablo R. Picasso and P. R. Picasso — though this evolution was neither continuous nor invariable.

We can find an occasional hesitation, an occasional return to the old form. It would appear, according to his own confession, that the influence of the Catalan environment was largely responsible for his final choice.

During the year 1902 his work shows some analogies and points of contact with that of Nonell, though these should be interpreted rather as a coincidence than as an influence. In Paris Picasso had already gone deeply into the consideration of female solitude, after his visits to the women's prison of Saint-Lazare, and he continued to develop this theme in Barcelona, where his friendship with Dr Cinto Reventós enabled him to further his knowledge of the subject at the old Holy Cross Hospital. For a time, however, he appears to have adopted one of the canons of Nonell, which was to dispense with the human face at times, and especially with the look on that face, in order to avoid the purely anecdotal and the problem of resemblance. He was applying this

principle, perhaps, in the *Two women in a bar* and the famous *Nude with her back turned.*

But this, for Picasso, could never be any more than another experiment, another adventure. For, attracted as he was by the human face, by the very humanity of man, he soon returned to them and had to come to terms with them — as was to occur throughout his life — sufficiently sure of himself to know that the search for the psychology or likeness of the subject would not distract him from specifically pictorial values.

Woman sitting, Drunk woman drowsing and *Woman huddled on the seashore* all undoubtedly belong to this stage in his development, and that is why I consider that it also includes his sculpture *Seated woman,* which was his first sculpture and was done at the sculptor Fontbona's house in Sant Gervasi in 1902.

Perhaps it was this life of material privations and of constant moral and intellectual testings that led him to draw the 1902 *Christ*; not the only one he ever did, but the most deeply felt of all. I cannot believe that his motivation was a purely plastic one. Although Picasso is a sceptic in the matter of religion, that

Christ reveals an evident self-searching. To this Picasso must have come by the roads of charity, which of all the virtues proclaimed by Christianity is the one most alive and deeply rooted in his heart.

In this drawing done in the stylized fashion of El Greco — whose influence he was pleased to acknowledge at that time — Picasso wanted to avoid any sort of conventionalism, and he envisaged this *Christ* as poorer and more helpless than other such figures: naked, in fact. As though he had not even a patch of clothing to cover his shame. From a feeling of modesty, however, the painter veiled the private parts, which thus seem to become yet another wound lacerating the body.

But Picasso was still thinking about Paris, for he knew that he was only going through a provisional stage in his career; and only his work afforded him consolation and satisfaction. In a letter still extant, which he wrote to Max Jacob around this time, we may read: "Dear Max, I haven't written to you for a long time. It's not that I've forgotten you, but I am working very hard. That is the real reason why I haven't written so much as a line. I show my work to my friends, the artists here, but they find that it has too much soul and not enough form...," etc.

In the autumn of the same year Picasso left for Paris with Josep Rocarol. This was his third visit to the French capital, but it did not last very long. In December 1902, or in the early days of 1903, he was back in Barcelona again.

35. 1903   Around the middle of January Picasso once more moved into the studio in Riera de Sant Joan which he had shared with Casagemas in 1900, and which was now occupied by Angel F. de Soto, alias *"Patas"*.

This period was to be the longest and most fruitful of all he ever spent in our country. The blue period developed, assumed various accents, and reached its highest point.

From the studio he painted one scene of the neighbouring roofs by day and another by night, as well as another picture of the surrounding streets, showing the bonfires the poor people lit to keep themselves warm during the night or early morning.

This was the period of the most intense self-searching in all Picasso's work. Blue is used, if not exclusively, certainly in preference to other colours; a preference which at times reaches the extreme of cancelling the few other colours used to complement it: green and yellow. Blue, here, is the plastic form of a search for the absolute: the blue ends by invading everything in his painting, to a point at which it becomes tyrannical. Jung has defined this period as a descent into hell. The subjects, indeed, are in accord with this self-searching, for they almost invariably evoke some problem or mystery of life: eroticism, fecundity, poverty, solitude.

This density exploded absolutely in the pictures *Poor people beside the sea*, *The ascetic*, *The old Jew* and *The old guitarist*. In these Picasso achieves a complete synthesis of plastic and sentimental problems, which for him at that moment were all one. It is a description of human wretchedness that amounts to an accusation, though the painter confines himself to description, without any sort of demagoguery. Of all these pictures *The old guitarist* is the one in which the composition seems to be most fully realized. The bent head and crossed legs of the model fit the format of the picture perfectly. Here Picasso finds on his own account (though

possibly influenced by the rediscovery of Romanesque art, which was then at its height in Catalonia) one of the great eternal verities of painting, and one which the Renaissance artists and even the Impressionists seemed rather to have forgotten: the fact that in any work of art, whether painting or sculpture, it is the model that must be subordinated to the composition rather than the other way around.

The existence of a series of drawings (some of them heightened with watercolour) dated 1903 and depicting country scenes made me wonder at first whether Picasso, in the course of that year, might not have made a stay in some village or country district of Catalonia that had hitherto escaped my notice. But when I asked him about it, he told me that these drawings were evocations of the time he had spent at Horta de Ebro. Particularly noticeable is a little old woman whose face is repeated several times. Finally Picasso isolated her from the other characters and made a masterly drawing of her in her Sunday best.

Contemporary with these tragic works done between 1902 and 1904 there is quite a large series of humorous or burlesque drawings, most of them done on the back of trade cards of the Junyer-Vidal brothers' firm. If the evocations of Horta de Ebro meant a way of escape from the dramatic reality that caused him so much anguish, these comic drawings are another form of pleasurable or cheerful escapism, another counterweight to the existential anguish of that moment in his life, a surely very "Mediterranean" defence against misfortune, as though he were keeping up his spirits with roars of laughter in the dark.

But the works which seem to breathe a warmer happiness are certain erotic scenes, like the *Embraces*, quite pagan in feeling but full of lyricism. While in the polychrome *Embraces* he had done at the turn of the century the bodies strained violently against each other, in these new works, in which the bodies are naked, the man always holds the woman's head delicately between his hands, as though it were some delicious fruit. But soon the thought of these embraces led Picasso to a consideration of their moral and material consequences. Then a couple appeared who seemed to be embracing more in sorrow than in love, as if they felt the weight of the Biblical curse.

For a long time I had been uncertain of the exact date of *Life*, that canvas which is the convergence and culmination of all these erotic and dramatic aspects of that stage in the evolution of Picasso's art. Though there is a sketch dated 2nd May 1903 belonging to Roland Penrose, which is almost certainly the one nearest to the finished work, I feared that quite a long time might have elapsed between this sketch and the execution of the canvas itself. I had also formed the idea, from something Picasso said, that it had been painted in the studio in the Calle del Comercio. But now I can state definitively that *Life* was conceived, prepared and executed, in an uninterrupted process, during the month of May 1903.

In "El Liberal" on 4th June, we may find the following note: "Pablo Ruiz Picasso. This well-known Spanish artist, who has been so successful in Paris, has recently sold to the Parisian collector M. Jean Saint-Gaudens, for a considerable sum, one of his latest works, belonging to the new series on which the talented Spanish painter has been working lately, of which we shall be speaking at greater length very shortly.

"The picture purchased by Jean Saint-

Gaudens is entitled *Life*, and it is one of those works which, even considered without reference to its fellows, is enough to make the name and reputation of any artist. The subject-matter, moreover, is both interesting and thought-provoking, while the artist's work is so powerful and intense that it may well be affirmed that this is one of the few really excellent pictures produced in Spain for some considerable time."

Of this extraordinary picture there are some sketches extant which show that the composition was very carefully worked out in concept. With it Picasso was endeavouring to give a message in painting which was by no means easy to convey. The man of the couple on the left, who was to be the principal figure in the composition at every stage, was Picasso himself in the sketches. In one version he is shown with his right arm raised, pointing to the sky. What does this gesture mean? And in another version the woman with the child is replaced by a second man, with whom the first is evidently having a conversation. What can they be saying to each other? All such possible questions might have remained unanswered if one of these versions

had been decided on as the definitive one.

But suddenly, while the picture is still being painted, a great change is made: the male model is no longer Picasso himself but his friend Casagemas. So now we can understand that Picasso's finger pointing to the sky meant that his friend had already died. Picasso, therefore, had been thinking of him from the beginning. The couple formed by Casagemas and the girl is being contemplated by a woman who, pictorially speaking, seems to come straight out of one of the 1902 *Maternities*. Her unexpressed reproaches are concentrated in her gaze. The picture in the background now appears without its easel, as a sort of middle distance to which a third plane of depth is added: a man alone, with nobody to talk to.

The couple in the foreground and the one in the background suggest to some extent two versions of Adam and Eve: the former fresh from their sin, the latter long after committing it. In this picture everything becomes ancestral. Today, as yesterday, the earth is inhabited by poverty and solitude. In this picture we have a sort of Pirandellian language *avant la lettre*. Picasso, with unusual daring, interrupts his

124. Mother and child in profile (Maternity on the seashore). Barcelona, 1902 or 1903. Oil on canvas, 83 × 60 cm. Galerie Beyeler, Basel.

124

125   126

description and offers it to us on simultaneous levels. I might add, in passing, that it was this same daring that was to permit the development of Cubism some years later. In the figure of Casagemas, Picasso forgot only what he had to forget in order to evoke it completely. It is a strange kind of Adam, wearing a sort of loincloth that endeavours not to interrupt the continuity of the nude...

After the painting of *Life*, Picasso's pictorial activities during the year 1903 and part of 1904 seem to have been mainly devoted to portraiture: the portrait of Sebastià Junyer-Vidal, that of Angel F. de Soto and those of the tailor Soler and his wife, Montserrat. The most extraordinary, to my way of thinking, is the *Portrait of Angel F. de Soto*, in which the expressionism that is always latent in Picasso's work makes a very definite appearance right in the middle of the Blue Period. It was from this face — and even more from these hands and the pipe — that the sculptor Gargallo was to take his inspiration, years later, for his rendering of the face and hands of the same sitter.

The portraits of *Benet Soler* (Hermitage, Leningrad) and of his wife, *Montserrat Soler* (Bayerischen Staatsgemäldesamm-

lungen, Munich), as well as the picnic scene that groups *The Soler family* in its entirety (Musée des Beaux-Arts, Liège), seem to have been painted with rather less conviction. The blue is certainly less intimate. It is possible that one of the sitters had a hand in this transformation, by leading Picasso in the direction of a progressive formalism which, as we shall see, was enjoying a certain vogue in Catalonia at the time.

For October of this year there is a working sketchbook full of sketches, most of them nudes, outstanding among which are the profile of a woman and that of a blind man, preludes to the painting entitled *The blind man* and to the great

128. The blind singer. Barcelona, 1903. Bronze, 13 × 7 × 8 cm.
129. Blue portrait of Angel F. de Soto. Barcelona, 1903. Oil on canvas, 69.7 × 55.2 cm. Mr Donald Stralem Collection, New York (unpublished in colour).

128

etching Picasso was to do the following year, *The frugal meal*, the second stage of which was carried out in Paris.

Of the same year (1903) is another letter to Max Jacob, which we must suppose to have been written in the autumn, for in it Picasso tells his friend that he intends to remain in Barcelona during the coming winter, with the intention of "doing something". This winter cannot have been other than that of 1903-1904, for in the following spring he was to take his definitive departure for Paris.

Then there is a drawing (Z., Vol. 6, N. 564), dated in the month of December, in which the approach to Gauguin's style is so evident that Picasso himself did not hesitate to sign it "Paul Picasso". This was his way of paying homage to the great French painter, who had died a few months earlier.

The dying year also saw the death of the art review "Pèl & Ploma", the last number of which (December 1903) featured reproductions of works by four artists: eight or ten by Casas, six by Rusiñol, two by Steinlen and a *Dancer* by Picasso. It was not much, but it was significant. At the early age of twenty-two Picasso had made his mark in Barcelona

130. The embrace. Barcelona, 1903. Pen-and-ink drawing. Vidal de Llobatera Collection, Barcelona.

131. The embrace (or "La joie pure"). Barcelona, 1903. Pastel, 98 × 57 cm. Musée de l'Orangerie Jean Walter-Paul Guillaume Collection, Paris.

132. Sketch for "Life". Barcelona, 1903. Pen and ink, 15 × 11 cm.

133. Sketch for "Life". Barcelona, 1903. Drawing in pen-and-ink and pencil, 27 × 20 cm. Roland Penrose Collection, London.

134. Life. Barcelona, 1903. Oil on canvas, 197 × 127.3 cm. The Cleveland Museum of Art (Hanna Fund donation), Cleveland, Ohio.

130

131

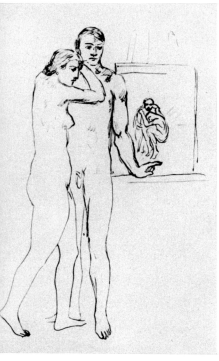

134

135. The old Jew. Barcelona, 1903. Oil on canvas, 125 × 92 cm. Pushkin Museum
      of Fine Arts, Moscow.
136. Page of drawings, with sketch for "The old Jew". 1902. India ink, 38 × 46 cm.

136

135

137. Sketch for the "Head of a Picador", Barcelona, 1903. Conté pencil, 14.5 × 14 cm.

138. Head of a Picador. Barcelona, 1903. Bronze, 18.5 × 11 cm.

139. The old guitarist. Barcelona, 1903. Oil on wood, 121 × 82 cm. The Art Institute of Chicago.

137

138

139

140. Sebastià Junyer-Vidal with a woman beside him. Barcelona, June 1903. Oil on
      canvas, 125.5 × 91.5 cm. Mrs David Edward Bright Collection, Los Angeles.

140

141. The blind man. Barcelona, 1903. Oil on canvas, 95.24×94.61 cm.
Metropolitan Museum of Art (Mr and Mrs Ira Hampt donation, 1950), New
York.

141

142. Portrait of Señora Soler. Barcelona, 1903. Oil on canvas, 100×70 cm. Bayerischen Staatsgemäldesammlungen, Munich.

143. The Soler family. Barcelona, 1903. Oil on canvas, 150×200 cm. Musée des Beaux-Arts, Liège.

144. The tailor Soler. Barcelona, 1903. Oil on canvas, 100×70 cm. Hermitage Museum, Leningrad.

142

143

144

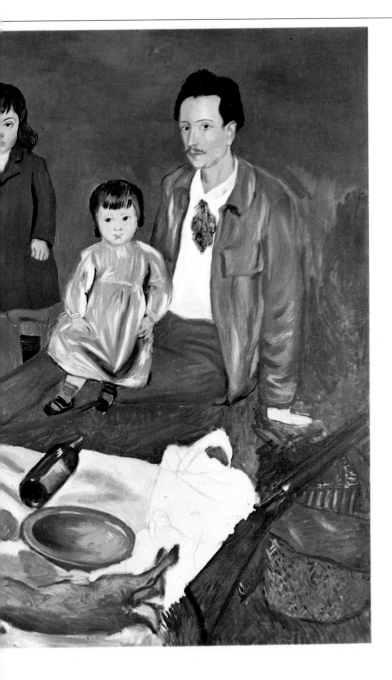

145. Christ. Barcelona, 1902. Drawing in lead pencil, 37 × 26.7 cm., according to Zervos.

146. The tailor Soler. Barcelona, 1903. India ink with colour wash, 22 × 16 cm.

147. Self-portrait in profile. Barcelona, 1903.

148. Woman's head. Barcelona, 1903. Pen-and-ink drawing.

145
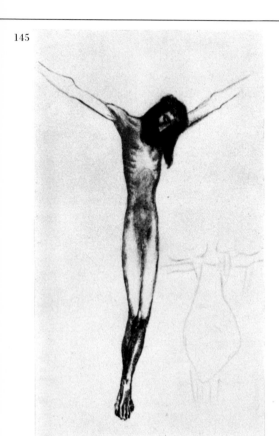

146

147

148

149. Evocation of Horta de Ebro. Barcelona, 1903.
150. Shepherd with his flock. Evocation of Horta de Ebro. Barcelona, 1903. Charcoal and pencil on Ingres paper, 47.7×59 cm. Rudolphe Staechelin Foundation, Basel.

151. Old woman in Sunday best. Evocation of a character in Horta de Ebro. Barcelona, 1903.

49

151

50

152. Family scene. Evocation of Horta de Ebro. Barcelona, 1903. Pen-and-ink
drawing with colour wash, 31.5 × 43 cm. Albright-Knox Art Gallery, Buffalo,
New York.

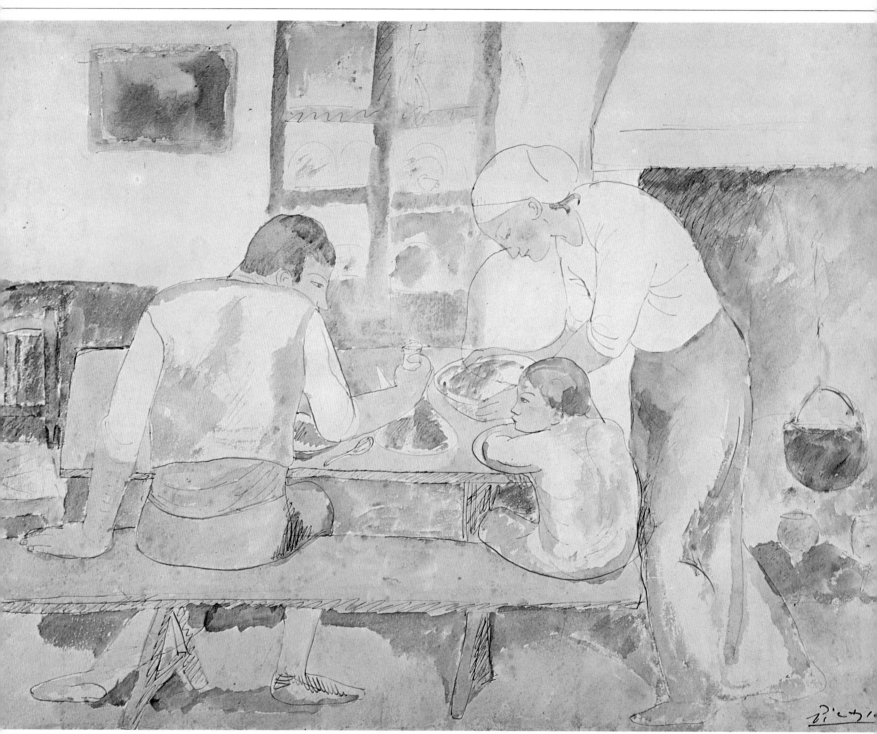

152

153. The poor man's meal. 1903. Water-colour, 24 × 33 cm. Galerie Beyeler, Basel.

153

154. Sebastià Junyer-Vidal with a lyre. Barcelona, 1903. Coloured drawing, 36 × 25.5 cm.

to such an extent that what had been the principal art review of the city, in its farewell number, included him among Barcelona's leading artists.

36. No. 28, Calle del Comercio. According to Sabartés, this change of studio was due to Picasso's desire to be more alone, so as to get on with his work in greater freedom, for in his previous studio, apart from his own visitors, he was often interrupted by those who came to see his friend Angel F. de Soto.

We know that it was in this studio that his father, Don José, prepared a large canvas for him, but we do not know what picture it was for. The two largest works done in 1903 or 1904 are *Life* and *The Soler family*. With regard to the former, we have just seen that it was quite definitely painted in the month. of May 1903. And the latter is generally regarded as having been done in the summer of the same year.

A series of drawings and pictures, known by the names *Poor People*, *Poor Wretches*, *Poor Wretches on the Seashore*, which are usually dated in 1903, must be considered to belong to the end of this year.

154

155. Sebastià Junyer-Vidal dressed as a bullfighter. Barcelona, 1903. Pen-and-ink drawing with colouring, 13.5 × 9 cm. Private collection, Barcelona.

156. Sebastià Junyer-Vidal, the painter. Barcelona, 1903. Pen-and-ink drawing with colouring, 13.5 × 9 cm. Private collection, Barcelona.

155

156

157. The madman. Barcelona, 1904. Water-colour on wrapping paper, 85 × 35 cm.
Picasso Museum, Barcelona.

157

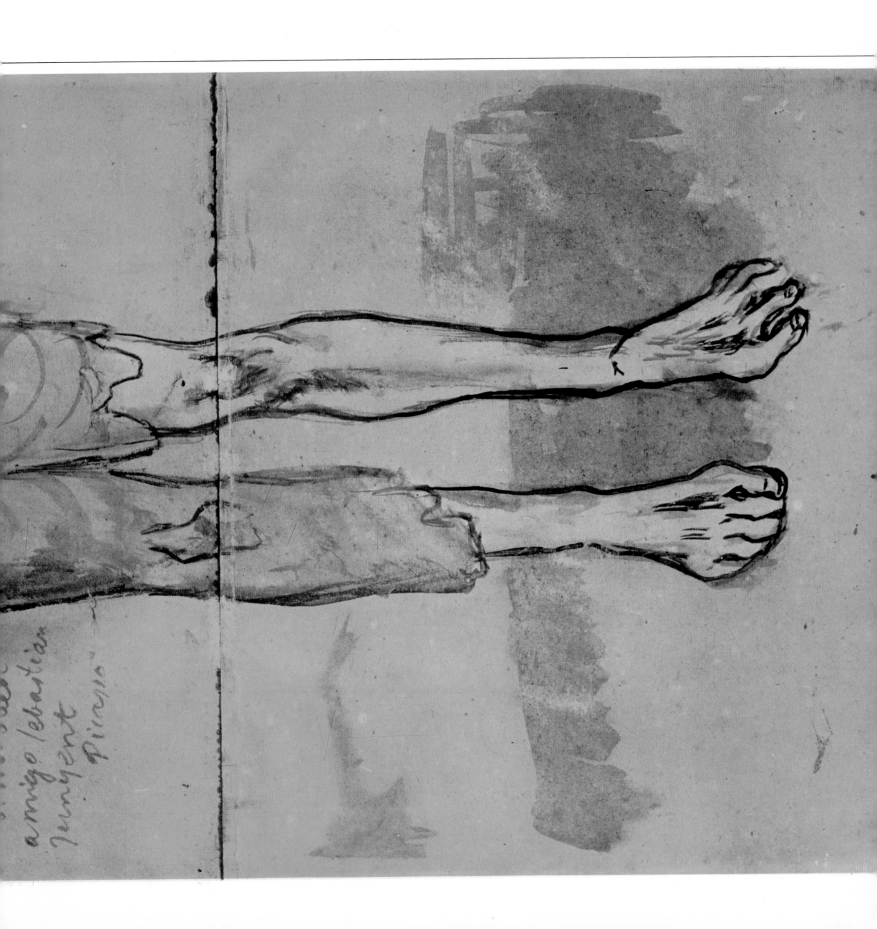

158. The poor people. Autumn 1903. Blue drawing in pencil, 46.8 × 36 cm. Heydt
Museum, Wuppertal-Elberfeld, Germany.

158

There is also a Barcelona townscape which contradicts the general tone of what is called the Blue Period. I refer to the view of the *Palacio de Bellas Artes*, with the sun illuminating the upper part of the building. Though blue is the dominant colour, it is surprising to find the orange-red of the dome and some other touches of contrasting tones — not so much because of the colours in themselves, which Picasso had already introduced in other blue compositions, but because the work as a whole breathes optimism rather than pessimism, freshness and vigour rather than despondency. When, exactly, was this *Palacio de Bellas Artes* painted? There are several reasonably credible hypotheses. Provisionally, however, I am inclined to think that it was done during the time Picasso was working in the Calle del Comercio, because this perspective of Barcelona's "Palace of Fine Arts" can be seen from a point very near his studio there. The brushwork, moreover, is very different from that used in his renderings of such townscapes as could be seen from his studio in the Riera de Sant Joan.

The formalism referred to in the preceding paragraph seems to have been accentuated in the last canvases painted by

159. Head of bearded man, apparently a preparatory sketch for "The madman".
   Barcelona, 1904. Drawing, 30 × 21 cm., according to Zervos.
160. Poor wretches. Barcelona, autumn 1903. Pen and ink with blue wash,
   37.5 × 27 cm. Whitworth Art Gallery, University of Manchester.

160

132

a) The Palace of Fine Arts of Barcelona, later demolished, which stood in the Salón de San Juan (now the Passeig de Lluís Company) in 1927.

b) View of Barcelona from the roof of No. 28, Calle del Comercio.

161. The Palacio de Bellas Artes of Barcelona. Barcelona, autumn 1903. Oil on canvas, 60 × 40 cm. Private collection (unpublished in colour).

Picasso in Barcelona. "Pèl & Ploma" had been succeeded by a new art review, "Forma", and in the first number of this publication there was an editorial by Miquel Utrillo which more or less said that form was everything in art, which was as much as to say that the form included the content. From the letter from Picasso to Max Jacob we may see that this theory or conception of the genesis of art must have been very fashionable at the time and that it certainly did have some effect on Picasso — not simply in the sense that it was opposed to his own ideas but also in the sense that he did make an attempt to come to terms with it.

The portrait of Lluís Vilaró is perhaps the artist's most representative work of this kind. In it Picasso seems to be endeavouring to paint simply the physical being before him and nothing else.

The nostalgia that seems to deaden the sitter's gaze a little, as though covering it with a light veil, is the only sign of sentiment or marked expression that we find in the work. Apart from that, it is the portrait of a perfectly typical Barcelona gentleman of 1904.

The portrait of Jaume Sabartés is still more surprising, since this was a friend whose face Picasso had already drawn or painted several times and with whom he should surely have felt quite uninhibited. This portrait of Sabartés is much more formal than any previous ones and, as in the case of Vilaró, the eyes are the most expressive part of the face.

When was this portrait painted? As to the year there cannot be the slightest doubt, since we find it inscribed in the dedication, which is in the top left-hand corner of the canvas: "To my friend Sabartés, Picasso 1904". But we are told by Sabartés himself, in *Retratos y recuerdos*, that the work was painted during the month of May. This statement, however, together with an accompanying one intended to supplement it, poses a serious problem of chronology, as will be seen.

Also done in 1904, in my opinion, is the celebrated picture entitled *La Celestina* (Max Pellequer Collection, Paris), though it has always been dated in 1903. Daix and Boudaille, however, have told me that on the stretcher of the canvas, which they have had occasion to examine, there is the following inscription: "Carlota Valdivia, 4th floor, right-hand back staircase, No. 12, Calle Conde del Asalto. March 1904." But these authors do not

161

162. Self-portrait of Picasso painting "La Celestina". Barcelona, 1903 or 1904. Drawing in Conté pencil and colour.

163. Sketch for "La Celestina", with S. Junyer-Vidal and a young woman. Barcelona, 1904. Coloured pencils, 27×23.5 cm.

164. Picasso with S. Junyer-Vidal and a "Celestina" in a tavern. Barcelona, 1903-1904. Pastel, 26×33 cm.

165. La Celestina. Barcelona, 1904. Oil on canvas, 81×60 cm. Max Pellequer Collection, Paris. (Ektachrome "Editions Cercle d'Art", Paris.)

162

163

164

Picasso

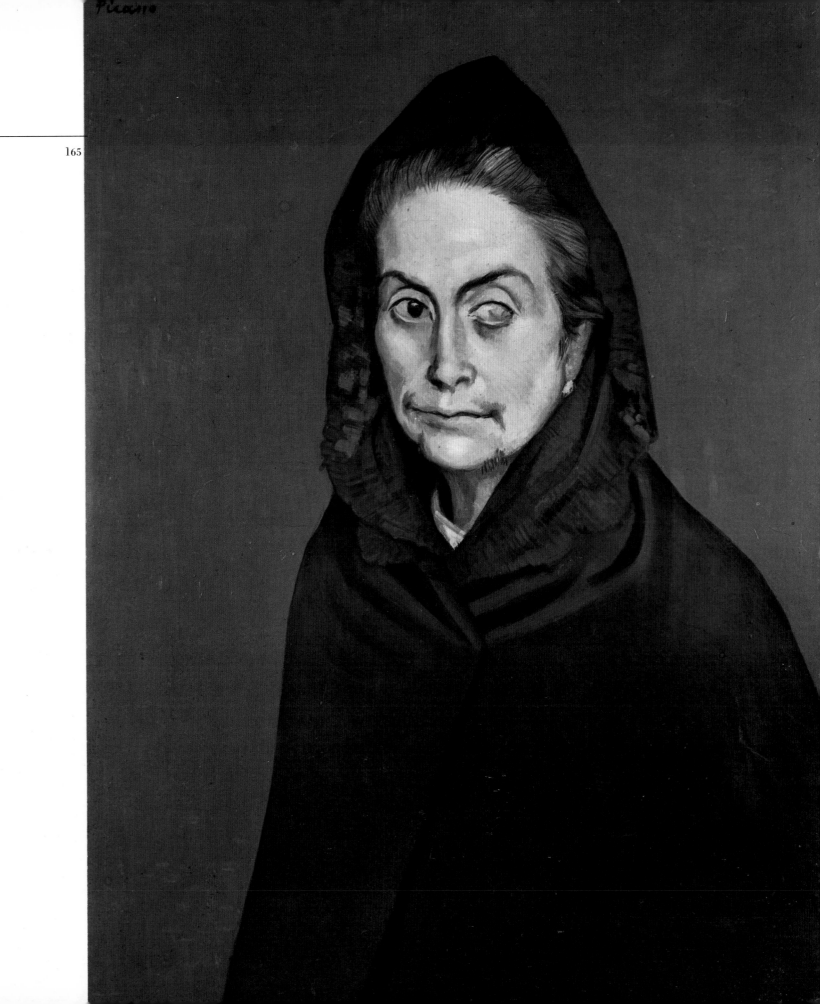

166. Portrait of Jaume Sabartés. Barcelona, spring 1904. Oil, 49.5 × 38 cm.
      Kunsternes Museum, Oslo.
167. Portrait of Lluís Vilaró. Barcelona, 1904. Oil on wood, 45 × 24.5 cm.

166

a) The house in the Calle del Consulado, with Sabartés' studio, which was decorated by Picasso, on the top floor.

b) The painter Ricard Canals, photographed by Picasso, who can be seen reflected in the glass.

c) Portrait of Picasso at the beginning of an article on him by Carles Junyer-Vidal, published in "El Liberal" on 24th March 1904 (unpublished document).

167

b

c

appear to concede its due importance to this inscription, resolving any possible doubts with the words: "The specialists agree that this work should be dated in 1903." Which specialists do they mean? Has some chemical analysis or X-ray treatment contributed to the confirmation of this hypothesis? Even if this were so, I should be inclined to ask for the proofs of such an analysis, for there are various indications, apart from the inscription, that lead me to place this work in 1904.

In this canvas we find the same idea of form as in the two preceding portraits. The character's head and torso are fitted into the dimensions of a medium-sized canvas, with a balanced distribution of the spaces. It is true that the portrait of Corina Romeu, painted in 1902, also fits such a description. But it would not be surprising if, even as long ago as that, somebody had suggested to the painter the advisability of "framing" the human figure in a more classical way, and Picasso, since his sitter was a friend's wife, had agreed to this suggestion.

An analysis of the blue in *La Celestina*, which I have been able to examine several times, and a comparison with the blue in the portraits of Vilaró and Sabartés,

might be a further source of indications of the date.

But to my way of thinking, even without these requirements I have more than sufficient grounds for maintaining my assertion. First of all, in the first *Sketch for La Celestina* that we know, in which we see the artist standing in front of his easel and gazing fixedly — almost obsessively — at the blind eye of his model, Picasso represents himself wearing a beret and a moustache, the same beret and moustache as we find in other self-portraits by him done in Barcelona shortly before his departure for Paris. Secondly, in another *Sketch for La Celestina* we see the main character with a young woman on one side of her and a man with the features of S. Junyer-Vidal on the other; and if we examine this portrait of Junyer-Vidal we will at once see that it is absolutely identical with the one on the first sheet of the celebrated *Auca* or *Aleluya* recording his journey to Paris with Picasso. The resemblance is so great, indeed, that there cannot have been more than a few days, or at most a few weeks, between the two. And the *Auca* or *Aleluya* was done in 1904, which was the year when Picasso went to settle in Paris for good. (Also by mistake, this *Auca* or *Aleluya* had previously been assigned to 1902 or 1903, since it was thought that Picasso's companion on his third journey to Paris had been Junyer-Vidal and not Rocarol.)

This second *Sketch for La Celestina* enables us to measure the distance between the original project and the execution of the actual picture. In the sketch the figure of *La Celestina* is still seen as something of a caricature, playing her traditional role of bawd or go-between. But in the canvas all trace of the anecdotal has disappeared: the figure of the old woman is now alone, blue on a blue background, while her face has become less picaresque and taken on such a serious air that it is hard to know whether we should call her *La Celestina* or simply *The one-eyed woman*, as the picture is sometimes called. Picasso, reflecting almost involuntarily the density of his own inner life, has also given density to this very human face.

It was around this time that Jaume Sabartés also rented a studio, on the top floor of No. 37 of the Calle del Consulado, a picturesque situation right beside the Lonja. The stairs leading up to this studio were so narrow that only one person at a time could use them. Picasso, as he had done on other occasions, completely decorated the walls of this flat. There was one scene that represented a Moor hanging from a tree, with one slipper still dangling on his foot and with a very noticeable erection, while a naked couple embraced directly underneath.

Picasso had been greatly taken with Zacconi's performance in the role of Othello at the Teatro Novedades in that year.

The celebrated "Blue Period", therefore, underwent an evident evolution in its subject-matter. In this Genesis, Picasso first created woman and then man. The family — or the "disfamily" — is the result of this union.

On 24th March, Carles Junyer-Vidal published a long article on *Picasso and his work* in "El Liberal". Space does not permit me to transcribe the whole article here (though it appears in its entirety as an appendix at the end of this book), even though it has hitherto remained largely unknown, perhaps on account of its length and unevenness; but I do want to quote certain passages from it which prove, beyond all possible doubt, that at the age of twenty-two Picasso had already acquired immense prestige among the artists of Barcelona:

"Pablo Ruiz Picasso! Here is a name which for many is less than unknown, for it should be clearly understood that even most of those who 'know' him do not know him sufficiently well to understand him or judge him."

"I declare, as I have said before, that to judge Picasso it is necessary to have a proper understanding of all men whose artistic output possesses transcendence and represents a sign of moral greatness in the development of the human spirit."

"Picasso is more, infinitely more, than many people — even among those who seem to know him — believe."

These words clearly betray the latent desire among Picasso's Barcelona friends to appropriate him exclusively or to be, at least, his favourite friends.

"That is why we see him taking 'harmonious' form as his starting-point and from it developing his inflexible, penetrating forces. And because of — or in spite of — that, he pays less attention to externals than to content, he prefers the inner life to the outer decoration; he is more 'religious' than idolatrous, more 'philosophical' than

'picturesque', more beautiful and handsome than pretty and flattering."

These lines appear to be intended to combat the excesses that that idea of form to which I have referred might have brought about to Picasso's detriment.

"Let it be borne in mind that Picasso's work should not be compared with anything produced in this country, it is something different. Get that into your heads, you intelligent laymen!"

The article ends with the announcement of Picasso's forthcoming departure for Paris.

But when did this departure take place? What was the exact date of this journey? According to tradition, it was at some time during the month of April — and in "El Liberal", in fact, I have found confirmation of this and even the exact day envisaged. The departure was announced for the 11th, but on the following day (12th April) there was a note which said:

"On today's express train the artists Messrs. Sebastià Junyer-Vidal and Pablo Ruiz Picasso are leaving for Paris, in which city they propose to hold an exhibition of their latest works in the near future."

168. Picasso leaving for Paris with Junyer-Vidal. Barcelona, April 1904. Drawing in pen-and-ink and coloured pencils, 22 × 16 cm. Picasso Museum, Barcelona.

This note (and, consequently, this date) would be definitive enough for me were it not for the fact that Jaume Sabartés, in the "Picasso chronology" included in *Retratos y recuerdos*, tells us that the last blue portrait done by Picasso was painted during the month of May and that the artist's departure took place "in the late spring".

Of course Sabartés, though extremely scrupulous with regard to everything he wrote about Picasso, was just as liable to error as anyone else. But what is surprising is that he should have repeated his mistake — if it is a mistake — by giving, on the one hand, the exact month in which his portrait was painted and, on the other, speaking of Picasso's departure as having taken place in the late spring.

There is a little mystery about this point which may be cleared up with time, but which for the moment obliges us to consider 12th April the correct date.

In the fifth number of "El poble Català" (10th December 1904) one of Eugeni d'Ors' *Gasetes d'Art* appeared, signed Octavi de Romeu, in which we may read: "Blessed are the restless, for they shall enjoy enduring peace! Mir, Nonell, Xiró, Ruiz Picasso — who is now preparing, in his retreat, works which will prove surprising and even frightening..."

Before Christmas, however, Dr Cinto Reventós received a postcard from Picasso in Paris, reminding him of his new address: 13, rue Ravignan.

It is a real glory for Barcelona to have been the scene of one of the great moments in Picasso's career as an artist, and to have witnessed the birth of some of his major works, but it is at the same time very sad for the city that so few of these works have stayed in their first home.

Picasso with Fernande Olivier and Ramon Reventós (left) in the "Guayaba",
the day before going to Gósol, photographed by J. Vidal Ventosa.

PART TWO

GÓSOL, 1906

1. Gósol, summer of 1906. Picasso had now been living in Paris for two years, in the celebrated Bateau-Lavoir. The Blue Period had ended soon after his arrival, and the Rose Period was already coming to a close. During the winter of 1905-1906, two important things had happened. The first was the suicide of the German painter Wieghels, who had been a frequent visitor to Picasso's studio, and who had taken part in the experiments they made there with drugs. The second event was the visit to his studio of the sister and brother, Gertrude and Leo Stein, who, on this first occasion, bought work to the value of eight hundred francs, a considerable sum in those days.

As his health, thanks to cold Parisian winters coupled with his privations and his experimentings with artificial paradises, was a little shaky; as he felt that the experience of the Rose period, so closely linked to that of the narcotics, was coming to an end; as he now, for the first time, had an appreciable amount of money at his disposal — for all these reasons, he decided to change the course of his life and his work and seek the antithesis of the environment in which he was then living. He would go to the mountains and change his style of painting. His money would last much longer in a primitive, unfrequented place. He had heard about Gósol from some of his friends in Barcelona, particularly Dr Cinto Reventós, who sent some of his patients there. Apparently, however, the man who really made Picasso decide to go to Gósol was a Greek friend of his, the son of a famous Greek politician of the time. When I asked Picasso whether his friend was the son of Venizelos, he answered cryptically: "Yes, perhaps he was the son of Venizelos..."

However it came about, we know for certain that Picasso arrived in Barcelona, with Fernande Olivier, in the early summer of the year 1906. We have a witness to this in that photograph of wonderful light and atmosphere, taken by his friend Vidal Ventosa in the studio they called *Guayaba*. Picasso is in the middle, with Fernande on his right and Ramon Reventós on his left. On the wall in the background there is the Casas portrait of Maragall, a photograph of Cléo de Mérode, Leonardo prints, etc.

Picasso's attitude in this photograph seems to reflect the state of his spirit at the time; on the one hand, a certain physical prostration (he is the only one leaning back, his two companions are bending forward), and, on the other hand, a faraway look which is still very sure of itself despite the physical exhaustion. Just at that time a monograph by Miquel Utrillo on El Greco was published in Barcelona, and not long before — during May — Maragall had published his *Enllà*.

May also saw the passing of the act of Catalan Solidarity, an event of the first importance in the life of Catalonia.

The line of the Catalan Railways which joined Barcelona to the Pyrenees, at least as far as Pobla de Lillet, had recently been opened. But to go to Gósol (in the district of the Upper Urgell, province of Lérida), Picasso and Fernande had to leave the train at Guardiola and ride the remaining thirty kilometres on mules. The road they followed was not the same as the one taken today by the occasional jeeps or other vehicles which venture this way, but one which went along the opposite side of the valley, the one which faces north, and was therefore practically impassable in winter. Gósol stands at about 1,500 metres above sea level, and I say about 1,500 because the original, medieval village of Gósol, now in ruins, stands on a hill which is about this altitude, while the present village, which stretches at its feet facing north, is 1,423 metres above sea level.

The village is not so tiny as we might be led to believe by the descriptions we have of it, beginning with that of Fernande. At that time it had 900 inhabitants, so it was no mere hamlet.

The medieval village of Gósol, totally deserted and in ruins, gives the effect of a lunar landscape, on account of the greyness of its stones. The modern village sprawls at its feet, like an unfeeling dog which has survived the ruin of its master's grandeur, for Gósol appears in medieval chronicles and documents as having been of a certain importance. The whole is situated in the middle of the imposing spectacle composed by the "Pedraforca" on one side and the Cadí chain of mountains on the other.

Gósol today is still a very rustic village. We may suppose that in 1906 the rhythm of life there was utterly primitive, as primitive as in Horta de Ebro if not more

so. Picasso took a room in the only inn in the village, which still exists, called "Can Tempanada." He probably had one of the two front rooms, for it is from them that one can see the silhouette of the ruined wall which appears in his sketchbook. This sketchbook, which goes by the name of the *Catalan Sketchbook*, was published in a facsimile edition in 1958 by Berggruen & Cie., with notes by Douglas Cooper, and it is of incalculable value in following the working processes and the plastic preoccupations of Picasso at this time.

On his arrival in the village Picasso had his head shaved, as we may see in the *Self-portrait* he drew a few days later. This detail is an indication of how serious he was about changing his whole mode of existence. If he wanted to achieve an aesthetic renewal, he knew that he would also have to effect a renewal of his way of life.

What is really amazing is the rapidity with which Picasso changed his colouring, his rhythm, his drawing, his whole vision. The models at his disposal were Fernande, the village itself, the villagers and the two domestic animals — the horse and the cow — which, with the woods, constituted the principal wealth of the place.

a) View of Gósol (1964), coinciding with the picture painted by Picasso in 1906. The church has been altered.

b) The inn known as Can Tempanada.

c) View of Gósol from the balcony of Can Tempanada. The house in the foreground dates from 1907.

169. Landscape of Gósol. Summer 1906. Painting.

170. Sketch from the *Catalan Sketchbook*, representing a peasant woman of Gósol. Gósol, summer 1906. Drawing, 11.5 × 7 cm.

171. Sketch from the *Catalan Sketchbook*. Summer 1906. This sketch seems to have been done looking at the outline of the village which can be seen from the inn known as Can Tempanada. Pencil, 11.5 × 7 cm.

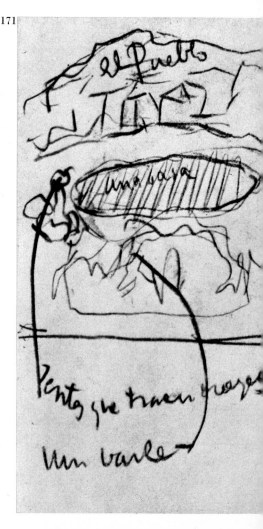

Picasso spent long hours at the farrier's house, which was also in the square, directly in front of "Can Tempanada". As in Horta, he enjoyed talking to all kinds of manual workers, or listening to the smugglers' tales.

172. Self-portrait of Picasso, shortly after his arrival in Gósol. 1906. Charcoal.

173. Swineherd guarding a herd of pigs. 1906. Pencil and India ink, 21×20 cm. Galerie Louise Leiris, Paris.

174. A group of pigs. 1906. Pencil and India ink, 21.5×27.5 cm. Galerie Louise Leiris, Paris.

175. Scene in the interior of Can Tempanada. Gósol, 1906. Conté pencil, 16.5×22 cm.

From his walks in the surroundings of the village Picasso always brought back some fossils, of which there were plenty round there, and of which he collected, according to his own account, two full suitcases.

The rusticity of the place and its people gave a certain rustic feeling to his palette, but his colouring, on the other hand, became young, ethereal, as if the altitude and the oxygen in the air had got into his colours too and given them fresh life. His principal preoccupation is with structure,

148

176. The two brothers. Gósol, spring 1906. Gouache on cardboard, 80.3 × 60.2 cm. Formerly in the Picasso Collection.

177. Sketch for "The two brothers". Gósol, 1906. Pen and ink, 29 × 21.5 cm. Dr Warner Muenstesberger Collection, New York.

178. Sketch for "The two brothers". Gósol, 1906. Drawing in India Ink, 31 × 23.5 cm. The Baltimore Museum of Art (the Fine Foundation).

179. The harem ("Figures in pink"). Gósol, summer 1906. Oil, 154 × 110 cm. The Cleveland Museum of Art (Leonard C. Hanna Jr Collection), Cleveland, Ohio.

180. "La toilette". Gósol, summer 1906. Oil on canvas, 151 × 90 cm. Albright-Knox Art Gallery, Buffalo, New York.

181. Adolescents. Gósol, summer 1906. Oil on canvas, 157 × 117 cm. Formerly in the Paul Guillaume Collection, intended for the Orangerie des Tuileries, Paris.

176

150

180

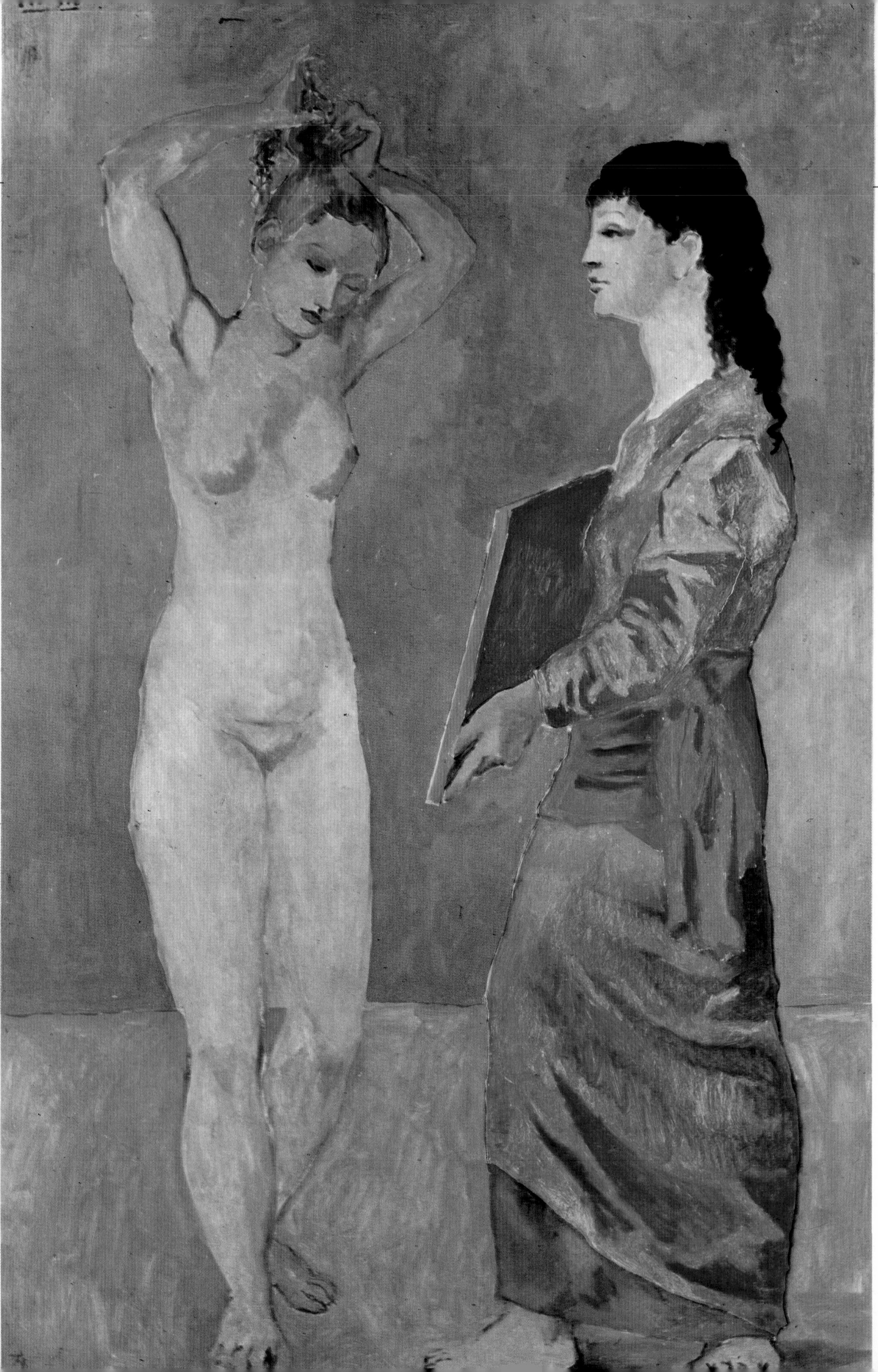

181

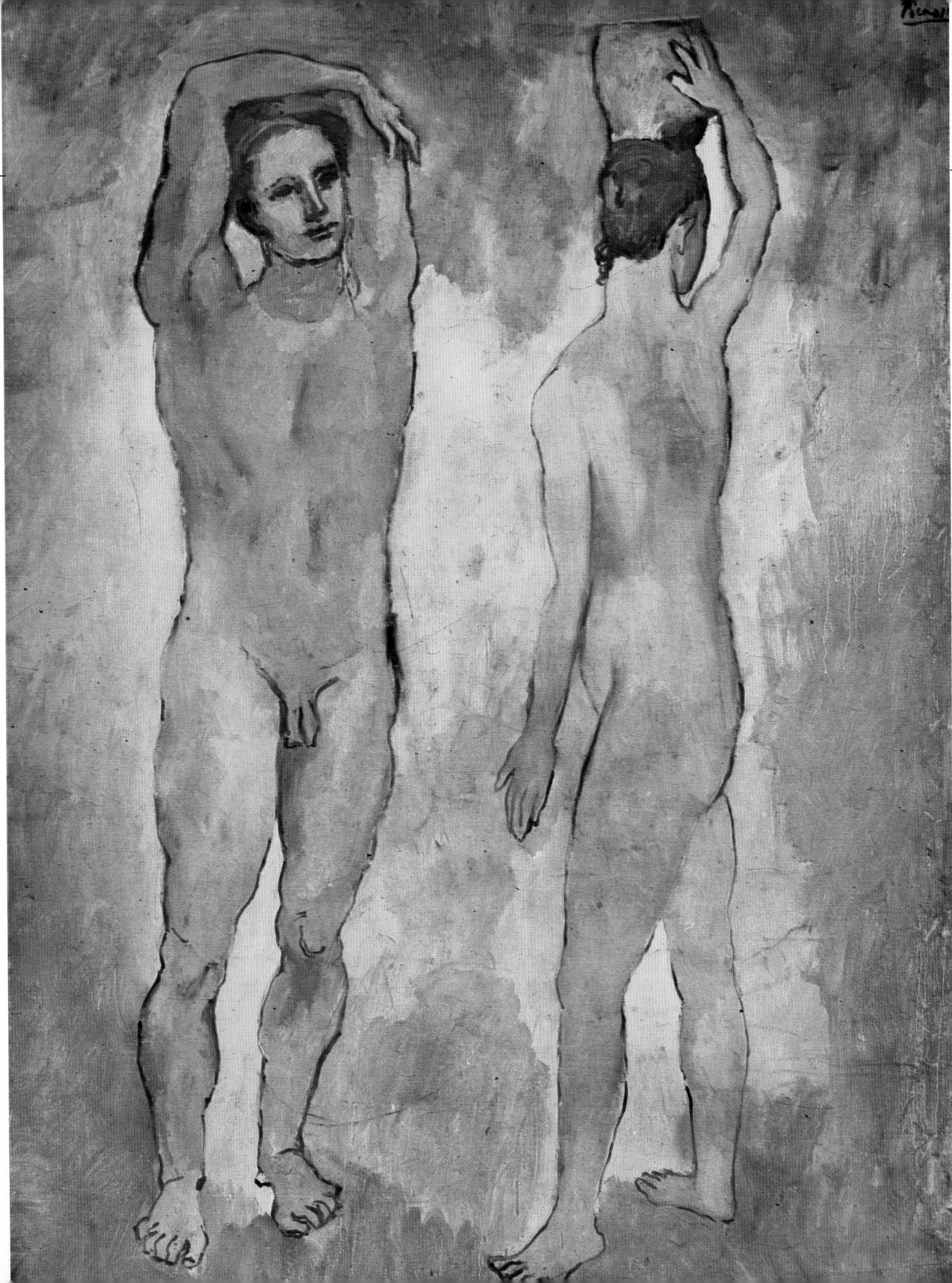

182. Double page from the *Catalan Sketchbook*, with a sketch for 'The three Graces' on one side and the copy of a poem by Maragall on the other. Gósol, summer 1906. The pages measure 11.5 × 7 cm.

183. The two adolescents. Gósol, 1906. Oil on canvas, 151.5 × 93.7 cm. Chester Dale Collection, National Gallery of Art, Washington.

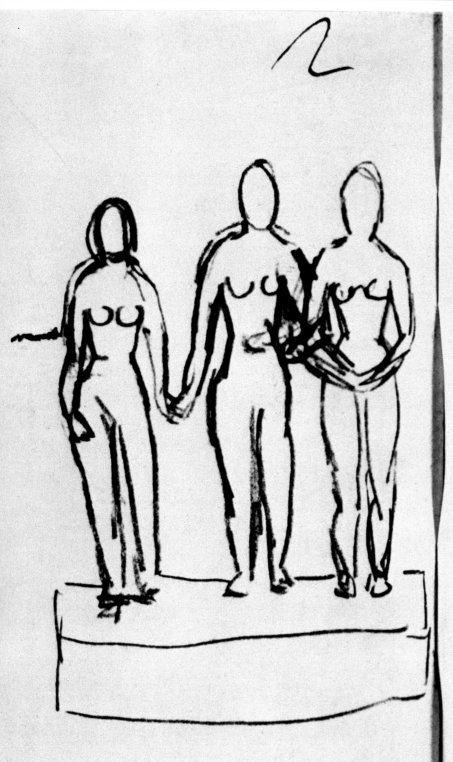

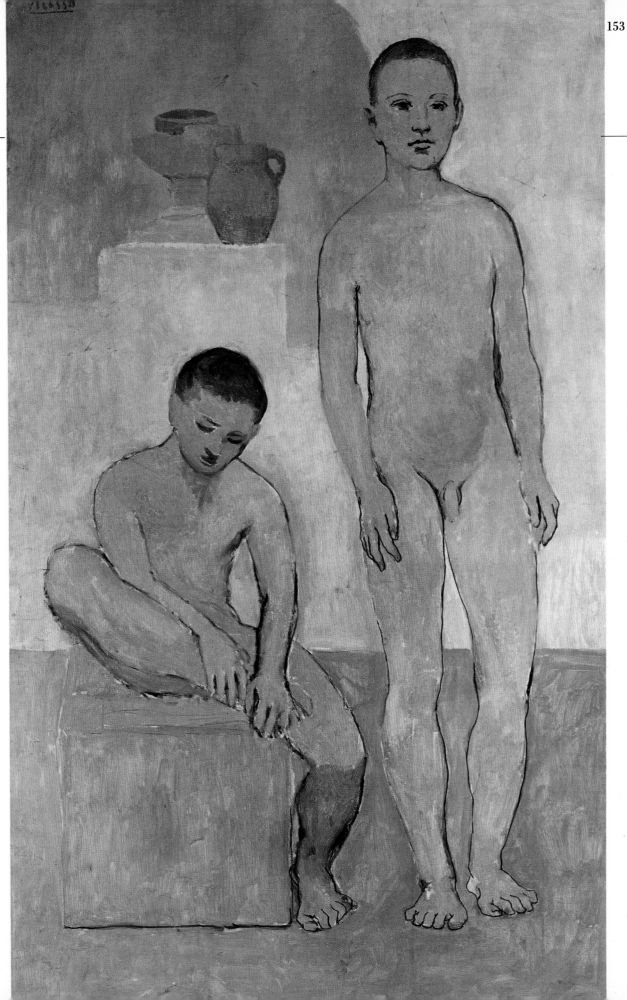

184. Donkey's head and dog curled up. Gósol, 1906. Wash drawing, 17 × 11 cm.
Kirchheimer Kusmacht Collection, Zürich.

185. Woman on a donkey, with the Pedraforca mountain in the background. Gósol,
1906. Wash drawing, 17 × 11 cm. Kirchheimer Kusmacht Collection, Zürich.

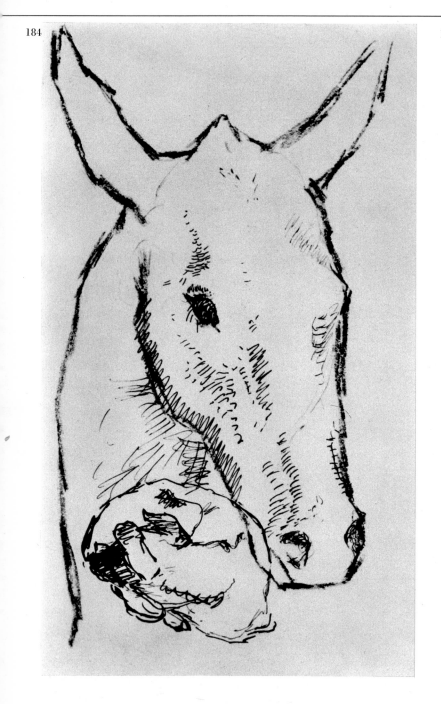

184

185

186. Fernande Olivier in Gósol peasant costume, with the Pedraforca in the
background. Gósol, 1906. Oil on wood, 81.5 × 62 cm.

186

187. Still life with *porrón*. Gósol, 1906. Oil on canvas, 38.5×56 cm. Hermitage Museum, Leningrad.

188. Still life with pictures in the background. Gósol, 1905. Oil on canvas, 82×90 cm.

189. *Porrón*, jug and grapes. Gósol, 1906. Water-colour, 34×38 cm.

190. Nude with her hands clasped (Fernande Olivier). Gósol, 1906. Gouache on canvas, 96.5×75.6 cm. Art Gallery of Ontario, Canada.

form, plasticity, quite the opposite, in a way, of his previous self-searching and metaphysical problems.

Picasso's work at Gósol presents us with an interesting problem, that of the classicism in Catalonia which was then in its heyday. As Alexandre Cirici has pointed out in this connection, Maillol's *Mediterrània* and the "archaic" paintings of Torres García were done in 1901. "Pèl & Ploma" had been replaced by another review, called "Forma" (the reader will recall how Picasso complained, in a letter to Max Jacob, that his fellow-painters in Barcelona found fault with his lack of form). And Miquel Utrillo went so far as to declare, on the very front page of this review, that form was the only essential value in art. That same year Llaveries painted the water-colour series entitled *Catalunya Grega*, and Marquina and Morera's opera *Emporium* had its first performance. Eugeni d'Ors, in his *Glossari*, paved the way for these ideas, which were to crystallize in the same author's *La Ben Plantada*, a veritable catechism of this new aesthetic religion. But this faith had even deeper roots in the work of the great poet Joan Maragall. Picasso had possibly already read Maragall's book of poems *Enllà* in

190

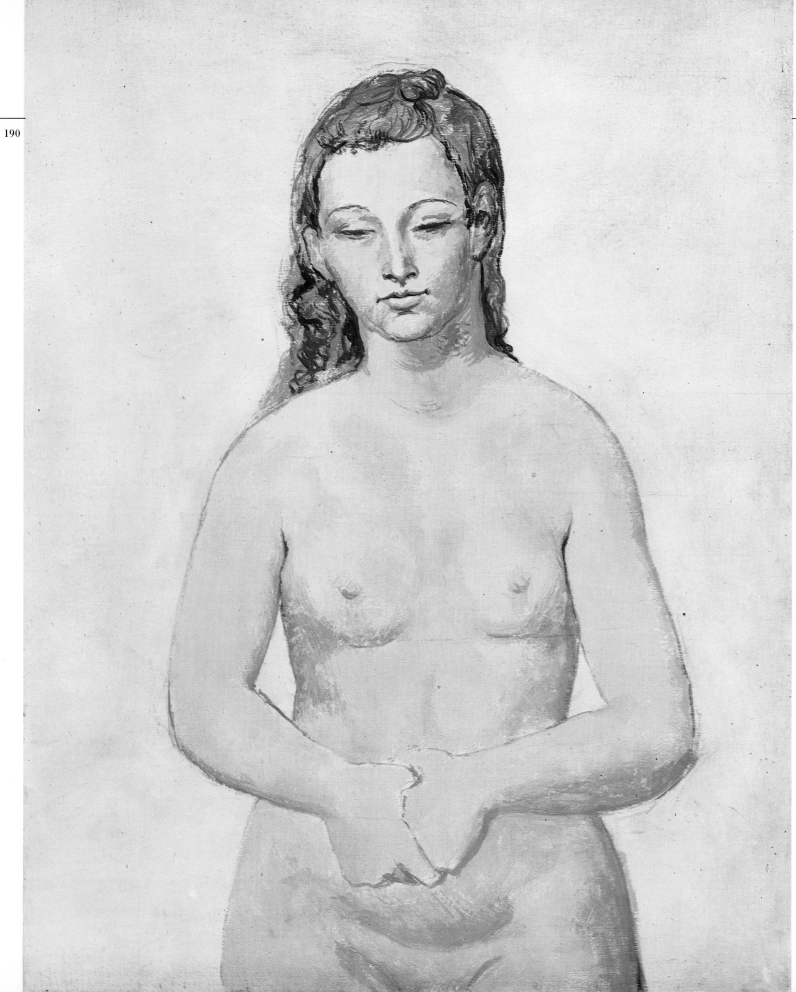

191. Bust of woman, full-face. Gósol, 1906. Pen and ink, 17 × 10.5 cm.
192. The Andorran women. Gósol, summer 1906. Pen and ink, 59 × 35 cm. Art
Institute of Chicago, Chicago.
193. Couple on a feast-day. 1906. Pen and ink, 21 × 12.5 cm.

191

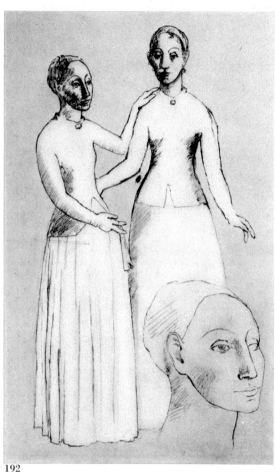

192

193

Barcelona, though he may have been lent it by somebody at Gósol. At all events we know that, in order to identify more completely with the spirit of its text, he copied into his sketchbook the most Mediterranean in feeling of Maragall's poems — the fifth in the series *Vistes al mar* — and translated it into French, most probably to let Fernande share his enjoy-ment of it. This poem, which appeared in book form that year, also dates from 1901.

Picasso's output while at Gósol is extremely diversified and cannot be pigeon-holed under any common classification. Among the various, sometimes very disparate tendencies to be seen in this work, however, the most significant — perhaps because it contrasts so sharply

194. Bust of woman in semi-profile. Gósol, 196. Pencil and gouache.
195. Woman's head. Gósol, 1906. Pen and ink.
196. Woman's head in semi-profile. Gósol, 1906. Pen and ink, 21 × 13.5 cm.

195

196

with his Rose period and with the works he was to do on his return to Paris — is what I would be inclined to describe as "Mediterranean classicism", since it has an evident connection with the Catalan trends we have just been discussing. This tendency culminates in *La toilette*, *The adolescents*, and the portrait of Fernande known as *Nude with her hands clasped*, as also in the face of one of the local women, undoubtedly somewhat sublimated.

In these compositions Picasso is endeavouring to attain total perfection of form, the ideal of beauty. Needless to say, he comes closer to this objective than any other painter — and closer than ever in his own career, perhaps because he had never before attempted it so earnestly.

197. Woman wearing a kerchief on her head. Gósol, 1906. Gouache on paper, 66 × 49.5 cm. T. Catesby Jones Collection, Virginia Museum of Fine Arts, Richmond, Virginia.

197

198. Young man from Gósol with his cap pushed back. Gouache, 61.5 × 58 cm.
Göteborgs Kunstmuseum, Göteborg, Sweden.

198

199. The woman with the loaves. Gósol, summer 1906. Oil, 100×73 cm. Philadelphia Museum of Art (Charles E. Ingersoll donation), Fairmount, Philadelphia.

200. Three nudes. Gósol, summer 1906. Gouache, 62×47 cm. Max Pellequer Collection, Paris.

201. Stylized head of Josep Fontdevila. Gósol, 1906. Water-colour.

199

200

201

202. Hairdressing. Paris or Gósol, 1906. Oil on canvas, 175 × 99.7 cm. Metropolitan Museum of Art, New York (Wolfe Fund).

This tendency towards classicism shows itself particularly in some of the sketches in Picasso's *Catalan Sketchbook*. Over and above this tendency, however, there is a searching for structure through form. Without this searching his classicism would have been exclusively naturalistic. With it, that same classicism was to develop into Cubism.

Picasso would appear to have had a presentiment of some part of all this when he drew and painted *The harem*, which might be described as a first version — though very different from the finished work — of *Les demoiselles d'Avignon* (which was to be painted in Paris some months later), and *Three nudes*, in which we may already see the breaking up of the conventional rhythm of the composition.

A typhoid epidemic finally brought this stay in Gósol to an end. Without returning to Barcelona, Picasso crossed the Pyrenees once again, following the paths used by the smugglers of Gósol, which was the itinerary marked in the *Catalan Sketchbook*: from Gósol to Bellver on mules; from Bellver to Puigcerdà by stagecoach; from there to Aix-les-Thermes, also by stagecoach; and from Aix-les-Thermes to Paris by train.

HORTA DE EBRO, 1909

2. Horta de Ebro, summer of 1909. In the summer of 1909 it was exactly ten years since Picasso had been in Horta de Ebro. As if to commemorate this anniversary, he decided to return, this time with Fernande, to that village where he had been so happy. The Cubist adventure was already in full swing.

At the outset of this new sojourn in Spain Picasso returned to Barcelona, where he was reunited with his family — with whom he went to lunch or to dine almost every day — and visited his friends.

The famous studio that an artist's model had christened "Guayaba", in which the leading spirit was Vidal Ventosa, had been obliged to move from its original location in the Plaça de l'Oli on account of recent town-planning changes; and this move had brought it to the very studio that Picasso had already occupied — first with Casagemas and later with Soto — at No. 17 in the Riera de Sant Joan. This was the third time that Picasso, though with very different characters and in quite another scenario, entered this famous house which held so many memories for him.

Before going on to Horta de Ebro, Picasso went to visit his friend Pallarès, who was then living in the Calle de Pelayo, in the building that now houses the *El Siglo* department store. Pallarès lived on the second floor, but his studio was on the top floor. It was in this studio that Picasso painted a portrait of his friend wearing a moustache — a portrait in which we can still see quite clearly the influence of Cézanne.

In 1909 Pallarès wrote to his brother-in-law, who was then mayor of Horta de Ebro, asking him to find lodgings for Picasso and Fernande. The reply, apparently, was not long in coming. According to Pallarès, who later on went to spend some days in Horta himself, Picasso probably lodged in some rooms rented from Tobies Membrado over the arcades of the square.

Any memories of Picasso's presence which still remain in Horta date from this second stay. There is a legend, surely based on fact, that every time Picasso saw a beggar passing under his balcony he took up a loaf, cut it in half and put whatever food was at hand into it to give

a) The upper square of Horta de Ebro in its present state.

b) The square in front of these houses in Horta de Ebro was formerly a big pond, in which they were reflected.

c) The upper square, painted by Manuel Pallarès, as it was before. The most distant house was the Hostal del Trompet.

a

b

c

to the poor man. On one occasion too, we are told, two ladies, scandalized on learning that Picasso and Fernande were not married, threw stones at his window, at which Picasso came out on the balcony, shouting and waving a pistol at them. However that may be, Fernande has said that Picasso, at that time, always carried a pistol.

During one of my visits to Horta de Ebro with Joan Perucho, Joaquim Membrado told me that almost every night Picasso, Fernande, Nicolàu Amposta Pe-

203

205

dret (nicknamed "Old Colao"), the carpenter Manelet García, Joaquim Membrado himself and sometimes his brother Tobies met together to play dominoes at the café owned by Joaquim Antoni Vives (now a hardware shop run by his son), who would play the guitar for them almost all night when he felt like it. Picasso, perhaps because he found himself once again in the place where he had learned Catalan, spoke in that language nearly all the time. There was a poor boy (the village idiot) in Horta at that time who, when he arrived at the café, always greeted Fernande by smiling and placing his forearm on the table with his fist clenched. Fernande would respond in the same way, fist to fist, and the poor boy was delighted. The assembly broke up when Fernande (who adored playing dominoes) was able to say, half in French and half in Spanish: "C'est fini. ¡Le gané!" (The party's over. I've won!)

Joaquim Membrado, who was born on October 20th of 1883 (just two years after Picasso), had, like Pallarès, exuberant moustaches, and every time Picasso saw him he greeted him with the words: "At your orders, Captain Membrado!"

Many years later Picasso told me that he always wore corduroy trousers in

204

Horta, and when it was time to pay for anything he put his hand in his pocket and took out a thousand-peseta note, which at that time made people stare. He apparently had quite a lot of these notes, and his stay was prolonged until all this money was gone.

One of the first pictures (if not the first of all) that Picasso painted during this stay was a view of the mountain of Santa Bárbara which he called *Landscape, Horta de Ebro.* In this picture, formerly in the Vollard Collection, the accentuated conical form is reminiscent of Cézanne's *Montagne Sainte-Victoire.* In thus paying tribute to Cézanne, Picasso assimilated his influence and at the same time freed himself from it, for the landscapes painted afterwards have already adopted a Cubist syntax which is wholly his own. They are *The reservoir* (formerly in the Gertrude Stein Collection) and *The factory in Horta de Ebro* (Museum of Modern Art, Moscow). Of the first there is a series of sketches, almost all of them in pen and ink, and the situation seems to be that of the lower square of the village as it is today — though now without that enormous pond which used to be such a feature of all the Catalan villages in that

206. The mountain of Santa Bárbara, near Horta de Ebro. Horta de Ebro, summer 1909. Oil on canvas, 65 × 54 cm. Formerly in the A. Vollard Collection, Paris.
207. The factory at Horta de Ebro. Horta de Ebro, summer 1909. Water-colour. Formerly in the A. Flochtheim Collection.
208. The oil mill. Summer 1909. Pen and ink, 32 × 17 cm.

206

207

region. In vain have I searched for the exact location of *The factory in Horta de Ebro*, which seems to be some kind of tile factory, as well as for that of some sketches in which — as in the painting of the "factory" — there are some palm trees; for there are no palm trees in the district. As a matter of fact, Picasso told me many years later that the palm trees were an invention of his own. The rhythm of the composition here is so very cubistic that the painter not only refuses to be dominated by the actual exterior scene but even, when it suits him, imposes his own scene, which he creates according to his own taste.

208

209. Sketch for "The reservoir at Horta". Horta de Ebro, summer 1909. Pen and ink, 11.3 × 14.4 cm.
210. Sketch for "The reservoir at Horta". Horta de Ebro, summer 1909. Pen and ink, 20.3 × 13 cm.
211. The reservoir at Horta. Horta de Ebro, summer 1909. Oil on canvas, 81 × 65 cm. Private collection, Paris.

211

212

213

214

In the *Portrait of Fernande*, too, which is now in the New York Museum of Modern Art, and which was also painted in Horta de Ebro, the beauty of this woman, who throughout her relationship with Picasso had been hailed as *La belle Fernande*, takes second place to the rhythm of the composition, to such an extent that we quite fail to remember that this is the painting of a beautiful woman. Only the painting counts in this picture.

According to Fernande Olivier, this stay at Horta de Ebro lasted four months, which explains the abundance of works by Picasso dated in this year as done at that village. The structure of the human face (almost always a woman's face) in the Cubist idiom recurs again and again, from the *Nude in an armchair* (Douglas Cooper Collection) to *Woman's head with mantilla*, in which the face fills the pictorial space completely.

There is also a series of intermediate canvases, which seem to be the various planes of one and the same object as though recorded by a cine-camera.

In some of the works of this period — in the *Bottle of Anís del Mono* (Walter P. Chrysler Jr. Collection), for instance — Picasso appears to be very close to

215. Nude in an armchair. Horta de Ebro, summer 1909. Oil on canvas, 92 × 73 cm. Douglas Cooper Collection, London.

216. Woman with a bunch of flowers beside her. Horta de Ebro, summer 1909. Oil on canvas, 61 × 50 cm. Wright Ludington Collection.

217. Woman's head with mantilla. Horta de Ebro, summer 1909. Oil on canvas, 39 × 30 cm. R. Dutilleul Collection, Paris.

218. Woman's head. Horta de Ebro, summer 1909. Oil on canvas, 65 × 54 cm. Formerly in the Paul Guillaume Collection, Paris.

219. Head of Fernande. Horta de Ebro, summer 1909. Oil on canvas, 61 × 42 cm. Kunstsammlung Nordrhein-Westfalen, Düsseldorf.

215

217

216

218

220. Woman's head. Horta de Ebro, summer 1909. Oil on canvas, 61 × 50 cm.
Formerly in the A. Vollard Collection, Paris.

220

221. The bottle of Anís del Mono. Horta de Ebro, summer 1909. Oil on canvas, 81 × 55 cm. Walter P. Chrysler Jr Collection, New York.

222. Front page for "Arte Joven", second period (1st September 1909). (Unpublished document.)

221

222

abstractionist Cubism, though this stage was not to attain its full development until the following year.

One possible result of Picasso's short stay in Barcelona this year was the short-lived reappearance of the review "Arte Joven" (second period), of which only one number is known to have been published. The drawing used for the cover was the one that had already served for the original review of this name in 1901. But the format now adopted the proportions of the drawing, so that the review now had the shape of an oblong copy-book.

It was, in fact, quite a different group that now tried to publish the review, since according to my information both Francesc de A. Soler and Alberto Lozano (the co-editor and one of the principal contributors in the review's first period, respectively) had died in the meantine.

This first and only number contained four drawings by Picasso, a head of Wagner by Torres García, a sketch by Remigio Gargallo and a caricature-portrait by Cros. There was also an article, signed by F. de A. Sorel (possibly a pseudonym for Angel F. de Soto), which was intended to present the new publication and to serve as a sort of manifesto.

CADAQUÉS, 1910

3. Cadaqués, summer of 1910. Picasso had often heard of Cadaqués, especially from Ramon Pitxot, a friend from the "4 Gats". Pitxot's sister, Maria Pitxot de Gay, was a singer and in the winter season she sang in Paris. But every summer she organized, from Paris, her visits to Cadaqués — but on a party ticket, passing off her whole family and any friends who might care to join her as members of her company; and, as they travelled with dogs and a parrot, it would seem that she had no difficulty in convincing the railway authorities.

In was in this way that Picasso and Fernande came in 1910. The train took them as far as Figueras, and from there they had to go by horse and cart to Cadaqués. This journey took six or seven hours, with two changes of horses.

Cadaqués was then a world apart; so much so that the villagers were more accustomed to speaking of Italy, France or Cuba (places which were accessible by sea) than even of Figueras or, of course, of Barcelona or Paris.

Cadaqués at that time was rather a poor village, living off its own natural resources: vineyards (for wine), olive groves (for oil), a little shooting and a lot of fishing. When there was a good fishing season, the women used to carry the fish to Rosas in big baskets on their heads, taking three hours to walk there and three more to come back.

In 1910 the house of the Pitxot family rose, bare and white, from the black, splintery, naked rocks of Cadaqués. The first trees in the garden had not long been planted, among them two little cypresses at the entrance, the traditional Catalan symbol of hospitality for pilgrims or other travellers. But it was not in this house (as I had previously believed, and as we are told in all Picasso's biographies) that Picasso and Fernande stayed. Both Mercedes Pitxot (Marquina's widow) and Ricard Pitxot have since told me that they did not remember having seen Picasso there — and Picasso himself, when I asked him about this, said that he had only visited the house. He and Fernande, in fact, settled into one of the village houses on the sea front. Soon they wrote to the Derains, who were in Cagnes, and who joined them after a few weeks. Picasso and Fernande went to meet them at Figueras, and in the carriage taking

them all back to Cadaqués that night Picasso played a little joke on Derain's wife, Alice, as she herself told me years later and Picasso subsequently confirmed. Apparently, when she struck a match to light her cigarette in the pitch darkness of the carriage, she found herself confronted with a bearded stranger who was laughing at her. It was Picasso, who had put on a false beard unnoticed by any of his companions.

At Cadaqués the Picassos, the Derains and the Pitxots often went out to fish or collect sea urchins in the Pitxots' boat, which bore the rather pompous name of "Nabucodonosor". One day Picasso's little bitch, Frika, refused to be left behind and swam after the boat, so they had to land on Es Cucurucuc, the little sharp-pointed island at the entrance to the harbour, to pick her up.

During this stay at Cadaqués Picasso did the etchings to illustrate Max Jacob's book *Saint Matorel*, which was published by D.-H. Kahnweiler in the autumn.

Quite a few of these illustrations are very close in spirit to some of the canvases that were painted at Cadaqués, and in fact they owe their being to the same kind of inspiration.

223. The guitarist. Cadaqués, summer 1910. Oil on canvas, 100 × 73 cm. Musée
National d'Art Moderne, Paris.
224. Glass and lemon. Cadaqués, summer 1910. Oil on canvas, 100 × 73 cm.
William Averell Harriman Collection, New York.
225. Woman with mandoline. Cadaqués, summer 1910. Oil on canvas. Formerly in
the A. Vollard Collection, Paris.

223

224

225

226. "Mademoiselle Léonie on a chaise-longue". Cadaqués, summer 1910. Etching
to illustrate Max Jacob's *Saint Matorel* (Plate III), 18.8 × 14.2 cm.

227. Nude woman. Cadaqués, summer 1910. Oil on canvas, 118 × 61 cm. Mme
Mérie Callery Collection, Paris.

226
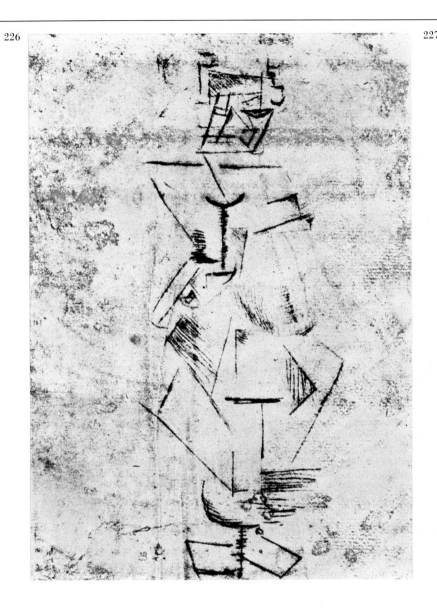

227

Picasso was now in the very thick of the Cubist adventure. The landscape, therefore, had an influence far above the ordinary on him. While Derain followed the paths of figurative painting (his *View of Cadaqués* is very well-known), out of all the immediate reality that surrounded him Picasso could only find some interest in certain forms which "did not disturb" his inner vision — or which, on the contrary, confirmed and strengthened it, like the prows and outlines of boats, or perhaps a guitar... We might, however, be nearer the mark if we looked for some explanation in the relationship between the sober colouring of the Cubism of that period and the landscapes where he sought his inspiration: Horta de Ebro the previous year and now Cadaqués.

Cadaqués today wears a rather gayer aspect than it did then, especially since it has become a centre for "la dolce vita". But its scenery has always been dour, dominated by the dark grey of the rocks, the mountains round about form a dissonant symphony of ochres and opaque earth colours, and the only soft touch is the silvery green of the olive groves.

We have now arrived, in this history, at the moment when Cubism attained the maximum disintegration of the elements of reality in order to reconstitute them in accordance with an inner rhythm, transforming them into lines of force, angles and bifurcations that co-exist with a sort of *pointilliste* counter-rhythm. If the titles of the pictures Picasso painted there are *Harbour of Cadaqués*, *Female nude* or, still more briefly, *Nude*, it is because those elements existed for him, even though they may have been metamorphosed into cubistic algebra. Cadaqués represents the moment of greatest abstraction in the whole of Picasso's work.

Before returning to Paris, the Picassos and the Derains went to spend a few days in Barcelona. According to Fernande, they took a fancy to a tavern near the port where the customers were served with as much ham as they wanted for nothing, but the ham was so salty that you had to order glass after glass of wine. It seems that on one evening there they all got rather tight on so much wine and kicked up quite a row.

Again according to Fernande, it was during this stay in Barcelona with the Derains that they visited Tibidabo and other places in the city which Picasso was anxious to show them. And it was also

228. The harbour of Cadaqués. Summer, 1910. Oil on canvas, 38 × 45.5 cm.
Narodnigalerie, Prague. Provenance: V. Kramar Collection: acquired in 1960.

during this stay, or perhaps the previous year, that they visited the sculptor Gargallo, who was then living in great poverty, and the sculptor Casanovas.

Picasso appears to have returned to Paris a little disappointed, with many canvases unfinished. Years later, however, Kahnweiler was to write: "... what is much more important, what really marks the break between Cubism and Picasso's previous pictorial language, is what was happening at that time in Cadaqués (on the Spanish shores of the Mediterranean, not far from the French frontier). It was here that Picasso spent that summer. He returned to Paris in the autumn, far from satisfied after weeks of hard work and bringing several unfinished canvases with him. But the great step had been taken. Picasso had smashed homogeneous form to smithereens. He had forged a new tool to help him reach his new objective."

CERET, 1911, 1912 and 1913

4. Ceret, summers of 1911, 1912 and 1913. On one of the last days of the year 1909, between Christmas and New Year's Day, three people tramped along the road that goes from Bains d'Arles (now Amélie-les-Bains) to Ceret. They had no fixed objective, but were looking for somewhere to end their wanderings. These three people were the sculptor Manolo, his wife, Tototte, and a lanky, blue-eyed boy called Frank Burty Havilland. They walked the seven or eight kilometres to Ceret, crossed the magnificent "Devil's Bridge" which leads into the town and decided to lunch at what is now Chez Dupont but was then called the Hotel Armand Janer. At that time full board in this establishment cost three francs a head per day, the food was plentiful and the water (which you can still hear singing in the streams around this smiling village) was extremely good; the air, too, was healthy. They decided to stay on for a while and, early in the New Year, they were joined by the composer Déodat de Sévérac, who had not been able to join them before because a new work of his was having its first performance in

The Casa Peraire or "House of the Cubists", in Ceret.

Paris. And so a kind of promised land took shape: Ceret, a totally unknown little village in the Catalan Pyrenees, was in time to become a very famous place to which art-lovers would make pilgrimages.

After they had been there for a year and a half, during the summer of 1911, Picasso, who had always been strongly atracted to Manolo, came to Ceret for the first time. For a while they all lived together in the *Maison Delcros*, today known as the *Maison Parayre*, in the Chemin de la Fôret (now No. 3 of the rue des Évadés de France), a house later to be known as the "House of the Cubists." Picasso had come alone. Fernande, according to what we have gathered from a letter, was waiting for somebody, probably Kahnweiler, to arrive in Paris, and came to Ceret in the month of August, along with the Braques and, possibly, Kahnweiler as well. The group had grown from four or five people to eight or ten.

In the "House of the Cubists" Picasso had a suite of immense rooms which opened on to the park — at the other end, as they overlooked the street, which was on a lower level, they were on the first floor. The cooking was done by Tototte, aided by Fernande and by Marcelle Braque. The company was completed by a monkey, probably brought by Picasso.

At that time Ceret was a thoroughly Catalan village. Manolo, who was a deserter, could feel a little more at home, could hear there his mother tongue; and the group could think of themselves as rebels against the established order of society and, above all, against the current Spanish regime.

Picasso's Cubism, during that first stay at Ceret, continues along the abstractionist path of the previous year, though a little attenuated and with a certain tendency towards the Baroque. The structures sketched evoke rather more concrete

229. The fan. Ceret, summer 1911. Water-colour, 30 × 22 cm. J. Leperrier
Collection, Paris.

230. The fan. Ceret, summer 1911. Oil on canvas, 61 × 50 cm. Formerly in the Paul
Guillaume Collection, Paris.

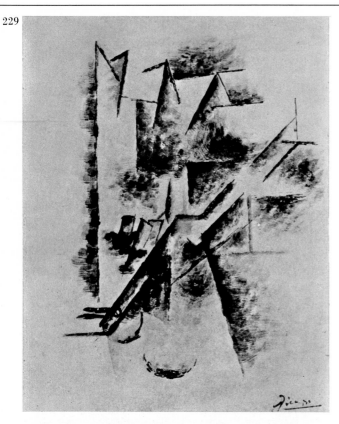

229

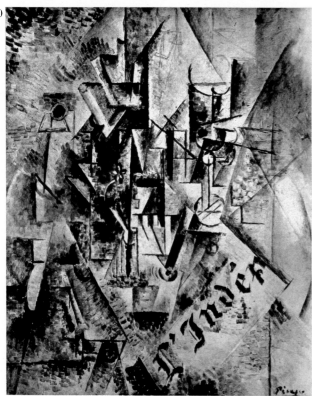

230

forms and seem to hint at certain objects of tangible reality. We might say that Cadaqués had been the highest point on the road to abstraction, and that here the descent began, though only very slightly for the moment.

This stage is known to some critics as *hermetic* Cubism. From this period we have *The man with the pipe*, one of the first oval Cubist pictures. Musical subjects are frequent, as in *The accordeonist* and *The clarinet*. I do not think myself that this association is purely fortuitous: in fact, the almost abstract language of the Cubism of that time was related to the almost abstract language of contemporary music, as Picasso well knew. The painter, with his brushstrokes on the canvas, attempted to create a harmony for the eye that would be equivalent, in Swedenborgian terms, to that which the composer tried to create for the ear. And it is worth noting that Picasso — eminently plastic and, as he himself confessed, utterly ignorant of music — was never again to dwell on these musical themes; for never again was he to come so close to abstraction either.

The problem of rhythm seems to be Picasso's main preoccupation in these

231. Character with pipe. Ceret, summer 1911. Pencil drawing.
232. Landscape of Ceret. Ceret, summer 1911. Oil on canvas, 65 × 50 cm. Solomon R. Guggenheim Museum, New York.

231

232

233. The poet. Ceret, summer 1911. Oil on canvas, 130×89 cm. Peggy Guggenheim Foundation, Venice.

234. Fruit bowl and fruit. Ceret, summer 1912. Oil on canvas, 55×38 cm. Alphonse Kahn Collection.

235. The Spaniard. Ceret, spring 1912. Drawing and glued papers, 62.5×47 cm. P. Gaut Robinson Collection.

233

234

235

236. The accordeonist. Ceret, summer 1911. Oil on canvas, 130 × 89 cm. Solomon
R. Guggenheim Museum, New York.

236

237. The bottle of Vieux Marc. Ceret, spring 1912. Drawing and glued papers, 63 × 49 cm. Musée National d'Art Moderne (Cuttoli-Laugier donation), Paris.
238. Violin. Ceret, 1912. Oil on canvas, 54.5 × 45 cm.

237

238

239. The violin ("Jolie Eva"). Ceret, spring 1912. Oil on canvas, 81×60 cm.
Staatsgalerie, Stuttgart.

239

240. Fiestas in Ceret. Ceret, spring 1912. Oil on canvas, 24 × 41 cm. Mme P. Sacher
Pratteln Collection, Basel.

240

241. Spanish still life. Ceret, spring 1912. Oil on canvas, 46 × 33 cm. R. Dutilleul
Collection, Paris.

241

Autograph of Picasso, half in Catalan, half in French, addressed to his friend Dalmau in Barcelona.

works. The rhythm has to infect the whole composition. And thus we see how the water-colour entitled *The fan* becomes the determinant rhythm of a more important oil painting with the same title, in which all the surrounding objects seem to be shaped by its influence. A topical subject, undoubtedly, for Picasso, since in the summer heat his eyes were probably used to the rapid opening and shutting of fans in ladies' hands — or even in the hands of Manolo, who was certainly not one to be debarred from using a fan by social conventions.

The bottle of rum and *The poet* also date from this stay in Ceret. On his return to Paris, Picasso was confronted with the unpleasant affair of the statues — just when the *Mona Lisa* was stolen — and soon after that the break with Fernande.

* * *

Picasso returned to Ceret on May 18th of 1912; his companion, however, was no longer Fernande, but Marcelle Humbert, whom he had rechristened Eva, as if to indicate that she was in reality his first love. They arrived from Avignon, where they had made a short stay. This new feminine presence was to determine, as usual, a change in his work; this change was that from what has been called *analytical* Cubism to what is known as *synthetic* Cubism.

In the spring of that year Picasso painted, either in Paris or in Ceret, various oval compositions featuring the shell of St. James. Before one of these pictures, the one called, in fact, *The shells of St. James* (J. Muller Collection, Soleure, Switzerland), Picasso later said one day to Jean Cassou: "I suddenly sensed all the smell of the port of Barcelona". We know, of course, that smell is one of the deepest of our senses. Though it is very highly

242. "Amics, cantem la ceretana". Ceret, 1912 or 1913. Pen-and-ink drawing (unpublished).

243. Girl's head. Ceret, spring 1913. Oil on canvas, 55×38 cm. Musée National d'Art Moderne (Cuttoli-Laugier donation), Paris.

244. Harlequin. Ceret, 1912. Oil on canvas, 88.5×46 cm. Haags Gemeentemuseum, The Hague.

242

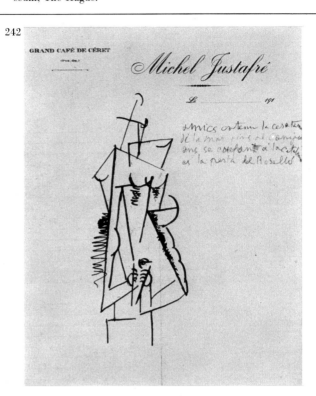

244

243

developed in certain animals, it seems rather to have died out in man; but when it is exercised, erotically for instance, it becomes one of the most powerful of all the senses. Rarely has Picasso expressed so vividly the ties that bound him to our city — above all to the district where he spent his first year among us.

This picture still bears — though hardly legible — the inscription: "*Notre avenir est dans l'air*" (Our future is in the air), just like another picture, bearing this same title, which shows us the initial stage of the amorous adventure Picasso was beginning to experience at that time.

Another canvas of this period is generally known as the *Spanish still life*, in which the oval is presented vertically and the figurative elements begin to pullulate. Not only pictorically figurative, like the bottles and glasses suggested in it, but literal, so to speak, like that inscription in which we read the first two syllables of the word "Barcelona", or the letters SOL SOMB, which of course stand for *Sol y sombra*.

We can find the same evocation of the bull-fights (which Picasso probably attended in Ceret) in the oblong picture called *Fiestas de Ceret* (Fiestas in Ceret), in which, apart from this inscription, there is another, half obliterated, which says *Entr aux aren* (evidently *Entrée aux arènes*, meaning Entrance to the bull-ring); in this composition the evocation of concrete and tangible things is even more evident and, in fact, from its structure, Douglas Cooper connects it with *Fruit dish with fruit*, painted there too.

The name of Eva soon began to appear in the titles of the pictures, in *Jolie Eva*, for instance, also known as *The violin*. However, on account of the reproaches of some of his friends — especially the Pitxots, who had brought Fernande with them — and the embarrassing situations which thus arose, Picasso had to leave Ceret, on June 12th, to return to Avignon and later to Sorgues-sur-l'Ouvèze.

It was during this summer that important personalities began to converge on Ceret — the poet Max Jacob, the painter Juan Gris, the Barcelona artist Joaquim Sunyer. One may say that this was the moment that saw the formation of what has been called (mistakenly in my opinion) the School of Ceret, in which we can detect at least two different tendencies: one traditionally Mediterranean and another Cubist or revolutionary,

245. Bottle of Vieux Marc. Ceret, 1912. Drawing and glued papers, 62.5×47 cm.
      Musée National d'Art Moderne, Paris.

245

which led one of the new visitors, André Salmon, to call Ceret the *Mecca of Cubism.*

For Cubism was gaining ground all over the world. In that very year the Dalmau Gallery of Barcelona had a Cubist exhibition, presented by Jacques Nayral and featuring Metzinger, Gleizes, Marie Laurencin, Juan Gris, Marcel Duchamp and the sculptor Agero. Picasso was not represented, any more than in most of the collective exhibitions of those years, but this very absence made his presence more inescapable: everybody knew that he was the prime mover of that whole movement.

The Dalmau Gallery had also held, during the month of February, an exhibition of drawings from Picasso's Blue Period.

*   *   *

In the spring of 1913 Picasso and Eva returned to Ceret, where they were soon joined by the Braques and Max Jacob.

There is an oval picture, painted in Paris on November 9th 1912, in which Picasso, for the first time, introduces a real element in his picture; it is the *Still life with chair caning,* considered by Douglas Cooper to be the first step in the adventure of the *papiers collés.* In this picture Picasso has stuck on a piece of oilcloth simulating chair caning, tremendously real, which is in complete contrast to the rest of the work and obliges us to see the painting in a totally new way.

The same fury that had brought him to the farthest limits of abstraction now obliged him to seek balance in the opposite extreme: to see and touch something real became a necessity. Here we might note, in passing, that this joint adventure of Picasso and Braque seems to presage, over fifty years in advance, one of the developments of modern art, in which the fury of abstraction gave place to the realism of Pop Art or other similar movements.

We have now passed from *pointilliste* meticulousness to a simplification of the painted surface, but also from one concept — that of disintegrating reality in the composition, reducing it to rhythm and lines of force — to another concept: that of reintroducing reality by a very different way from that by which it had left. By fixing papers, pieces of cloth or sand — elements we regard as real in our everyday life — on to the composition, we

246. Ceret, 1913. Glued papers, charcoal and pastel, 47.7 × 63 cm.

246

break the unity of this composition, a unity established as inviolable by all prevailing canons since the Renaissance. This forces the eye to look at things afresh, which is what Picasso and Braque had set themselves to do at this time. At the same time, as Roland Penrose says, the most real elements become the most virtual ones, because they are false (the caning painted on the oilcloth is false caning), and those which are apparently most virtual (the pipe, the glass, the slice of lemon, which are hinted at), become the most real elements because they are independent, they have a life of their own, they are entities created by the artist. As Barr has said, we move from aesthetics into the field of metaphysical speculation.

The year 1913 marked the apogee of the collage, and many of these, now famous, were done here: *Glass and bottle of Bass* (Guggenheim Foundation, New York), *Glass and bottle on a table* (G. L. K. Morris, New York), *Playing card and glass* (Marthe Heunebert Collection, Paris), *Musical instruments* (Museum of Modern Art, Moscow).

Ceret (collage, charcoal and pastel) is a picture quite apart from the others, a work of unequalled youthfulness and optimism. We might almost describe it as a ballet in which the elements of the décor (houses, trees, letters, colours) had become actors and started dancing before our astonished eyes. At the same time *Ceret* indicates a return "in advance" to reality... And when the return actually takes place, it cannot be properly judged without taking this composition very much into consideration.

From Ceret Picasso made one sortie into Spain, as far as Figueras, possibly to attend a bullfight. But the death of his father in May of this year (which had obliged him to return to Barcelona) and now Eva's illness, which had been growing worse all this time, soon brought about a profound transformation in his art. It appears that on his way back from Barcelona, with Eva and Max Jacob, he stopped for a day to visit Gerona.

BARCELONA, 1917

5. Barcelona, 1917. During his sojourns in Ceret, and above all after the death of his father, Picasso is known to have made frequent journeys to Barcelona to see his family. But so far I have not been able to find reliable proof of these visits.

I can, however, speak with certainty of the two stays he made in Barcelona during the year 1917.

The first of these probably began, in fact, during the 1916 Christmas holidays. It should be remembered that Picasso had lost Eva (Marcelle Humbert) during the previous year, that many of his friends (among them Braque, Derain, Apollinaire and Salmon) had been called up and were at the front, and that he was going through a period of solitude and emptiness.

On 4th January 1917 the Catalan weekly "L'Esquella de la Torratxa" printed four unpublished drawings by Picasso. Why should they publish these drawings, or remind their readers of the artist's work, if it were not because Picasso was actually in Barcelona at the time? The drawings reproduced all came from San-tiago Rusiñol's collection at the Cau Ferrat in Sitges.

But the real confirmation of my hypothesis is to be found in a letter sent by Picasso to Apollinaire, which is dated at Barcelona on 16th January 1917. The text is the following:

"Dear Guillaume,

I feel too sick of everything. Of finding myself still here. I don't know when I will be returning. But I am working. Don't be angry if I don't write to you, but you are always in my thoughts. Write to me if you want to make me happy. I met Picabia at the bullfight on Sunday.

Yours, Picasso.

P.S. My love to Ruby."

We know, of course, that Picabia was in Barcelona at the time, for it was there that he published the review *391*.

This letter, moreover, both in its reference to past time ("Of finding myself still here") and in its allusion to the future ("I don't know when I will be returning"), may well lead us to suppose that Picasso had then been in Barcelona for quite a few days and that his correspondent knew this; and it also suggests that the date of his departure was not exactly the day after writing these lines... We may conjec-

The Columbus Monument and the mountain of Montjuïc in the background, as seen from a balcony of the former Pension Ranzini (unpublished document).

247. Olga seated on the balcony of the Pension Ranzini. Barcelona, 1917. Lead pencil, 23 × 15.5 cm.

248. Olga writing on the balcony of the Pension Ranzini. Barcelona, 1917. Lead pencil, 23 × 15.5 cm.

247

248

ture, therefore, that his stay lasted about a month.

In this letter, too, Picasso says: "But I am working." So what were the works that he did in Barcelona during this stay? We know that his output in the year 1917 was of two kinds: Cubist and figurative. If we were to go by mere hypothesis, we might be inclined to say that the first were done in January and the second during the following spring. But if we examine all that he did a little more carefully, we shall see that between the more figurative and the more abstract works there are certain connections, almost as though Picasso had wished to let us see that they were all done

249. Olga, in profile. Barcelona, 1917. Lead pencil, 23 × 15.5 cm.
250. Olga wearing a Spanish mantilla. Barcelona, 1917. Oil on canvas. Formerly in the Picasso Collection.

at the same time. In *Fruit bowl with fruit* we see the same fruit bowl as is held in the hand of the *Character at table*. And in *Barcelona composition* the silvery greys of the Venetian blinds at the sides are exactly the same as we find in some of the Cubist or almost abstract compositions. It is possible, therefore, that in the Picasso catalogue there are other canvases and drawings, not precisely dated, which were done in Barcelona during the month of January 1917.

One of the clues on which I was relying to help me clarify this point was that of the performances given in Barcelona by Blanquita Suárez. But my research into

Picasso in the Galeries Laietanes, Barcelona, in 1917. At his feet: Mateo F. de
Soto, Seated: Maeztu, Picasso, Iturrino, Behind, left to right: Padilla, Feliu
Elies, Romà Jori, Xavier Nogués, Soglio, M. Humbert, Plandiura, A. Riera,
G. Anyés, J. Colomer, Ricard Canals, Background: Miquel Utrillo, S. Segura
and Aragay.

this has proved useless, for this famous dancer opened at the Teatro Tívoli on 20th January (at which date Picasso was probably still in Barcelona) and, after a fairly long season and an absence of a few months, brought her show back to the same theatre on 28th June, when Picasso, too, had returned to the city.

(I should perhaps inform the reader that Blanquita Suárez, who was billed as a "comic soprano", had become one of the idols of the public thanks to her performances in pieces with such fascinating titles as *The island of pleasures, The wonder of Damascus* and *The white kitten*. We learn from the press that on 12th July 1917 Blanquita gave her farewell performance in this *genre*, since she wished "to devote her talents to popular Spanish songs". Her name, even in the official entertainment guides in newspapers, was almost always accompanied by some enthusiastic word of description. Thus, in the advertisement for her company that appeared on 30th June we read:

"Blanquita's greatest triumph: *The island of pleasures*. What a telephonist Blanquita makes! What a doll, this Blanquita! What gaiety she brings us, our Blanquita!").

In 1917, at all events, Picasso returned to Paris; but we know that on 17th February he and Jean Cocteau left Paris for Rome, where they were going to prepare the first performance of *Parade*.

After this preparation in Rome the ballet *Parade* — written by Cocteau, with music by Satie, choreography by Massine and décor by Picasso — had its first performance in Paris that same year. As everybody knows, this first performance created an uproar, and it took all the authority of Apollinaire, a war hero wounded at the front (who in presenting this work used the term Surrealism for the first time), to pacify the audience.

The décor consisted of a drop curtain of over 10 metres by 17, on which the characters —two harlequins, a columbine, a negro, a bullfighter, etc.— are presented in intelligible language, reminding one, in some aspects, of the Rose or Blue-Rose period, though more sharply defined, more concrete. The scandal, however, was not caused by these figures, but by a pair of extraordinary figures, conceived as elements of Cubist architecture, rather like a house of cards, but able to move on the stage. These were the *Ménager de Paris* and the *Ménager de New York*.

251

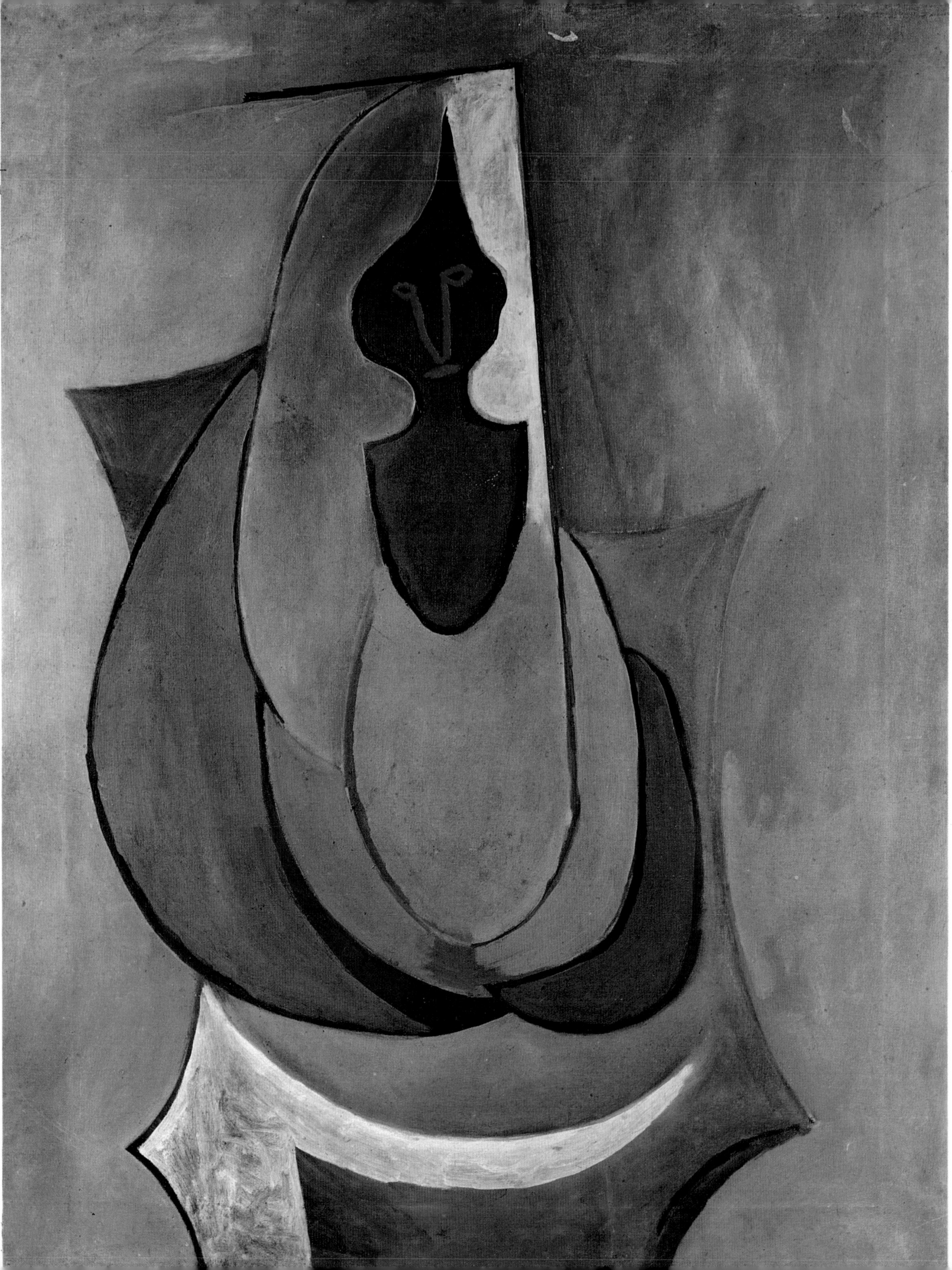

253

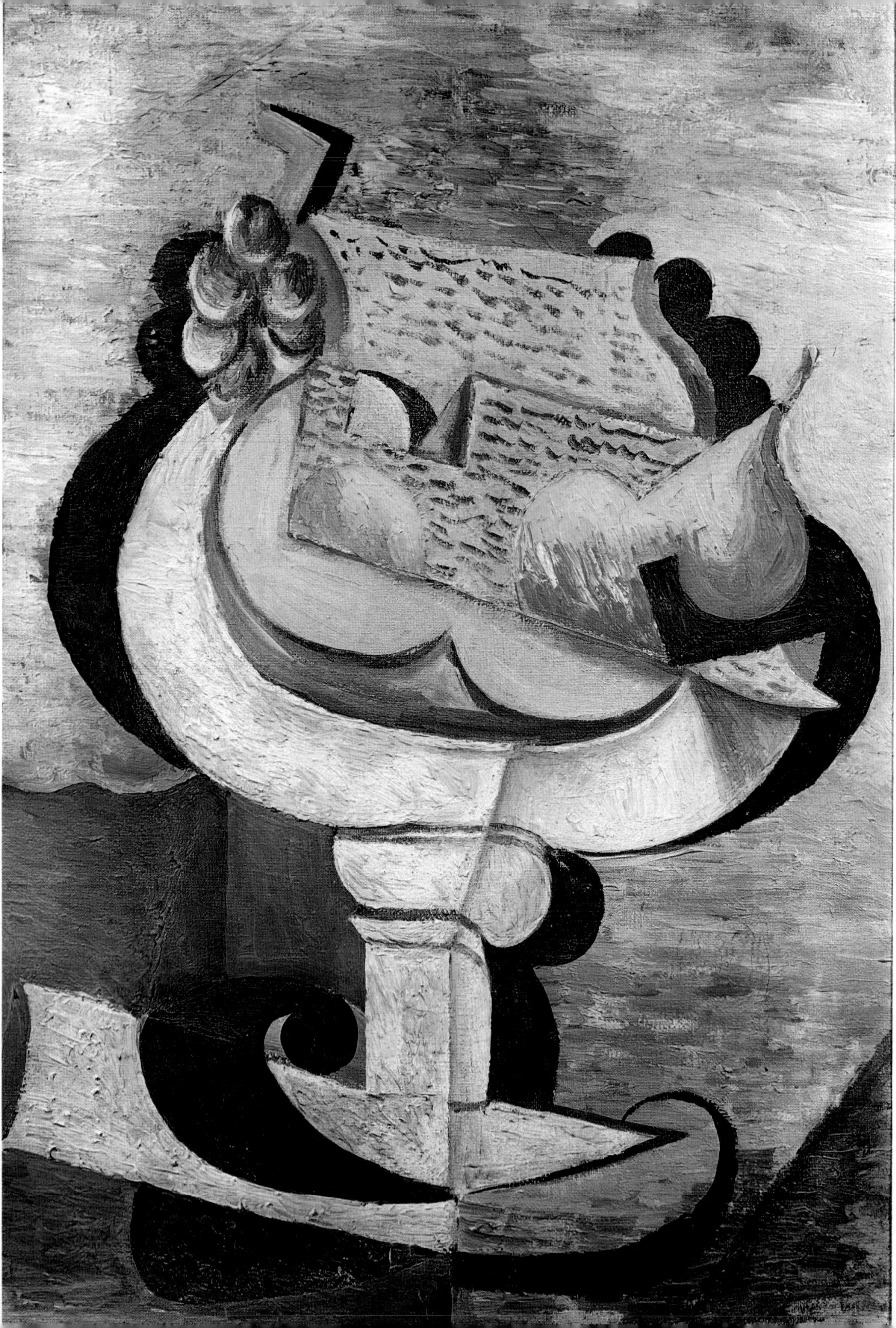

254

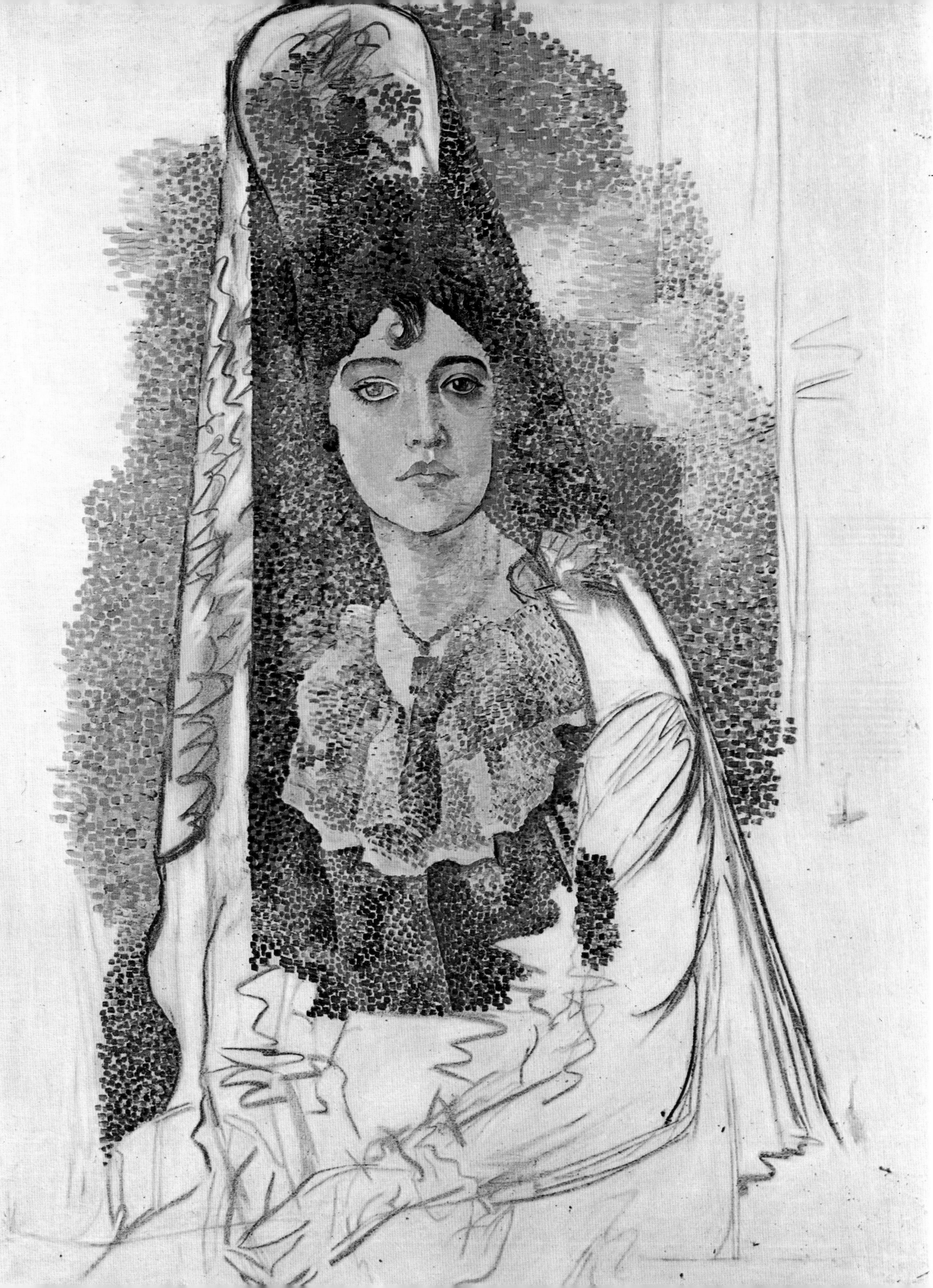

255. Blanquita Suárez. Barcelona, 1917. Oil on canvas, 108×60 cm. Picasso Museum, Barcelona.

255

Picasso arrived in Barcelona from Madrid in the month of June 1917, following Diaghilev's Russian Ballet Company.

This time Picasso returned to Barcelona in a very different spirit from that which had governed his previous visits: it was a spirit of triumph. His name had gone beyond the merely local and had become, definitively, universal.

In Diaghilev's company there was a young dancer, Olga Koklova, daughter of a Russian general, who had stolen Picasso's heart. Really he was following her as much as the company, or perhaps more.

We must not forget that all this was in the middle of the First World War, and that Spain was neutral. In this connection the Russian Ballet was seeking, and found, a haven of peace, though even in Spain there was a marked division between Francophiles and Germanophiles.

The Russian Ballet Company established itself in the *"Gran Teatro del Liceo"*, Barcelona's opera house, and gave a series of performances there between the 23rd and 30th of June, with such works as *Sylphides, Carnaval, Prince Igor*, etc. The director was the implacable Diaghilev, and among the dancers were Nijinsky and Massine.

256. Gonzalo de Maeztu. Barcelona, June 1917. Pencil drawing, 39×32 cm.
Torelló Collection, Barcelona.
257. The balcony (Barcelona composition with the Columbus monument in the
background.) Barcelona, 1917. Oil on canvas, 39×33 cm. Picasso Museum,
Barcelona.

257

258. The cock canary and the little hen canary. Barcelona, 21st July 1917. Pen and ink on paper. Andreu Collection, Barcelona.

259. Bullfight. Barcelona, 1917. Lead pencil, 23 × 15.5 cm.

260. Bullfight. Barcelona, 1917. Lead pencil, 23 × 15.5 cm.

261. Bullfight. Barcelona, 1917. Lead pencil, 23 × 15.5 cm.

262. Bullfight. Barcelona, 1917. Lead pencil, 23 × 15.5 cm.

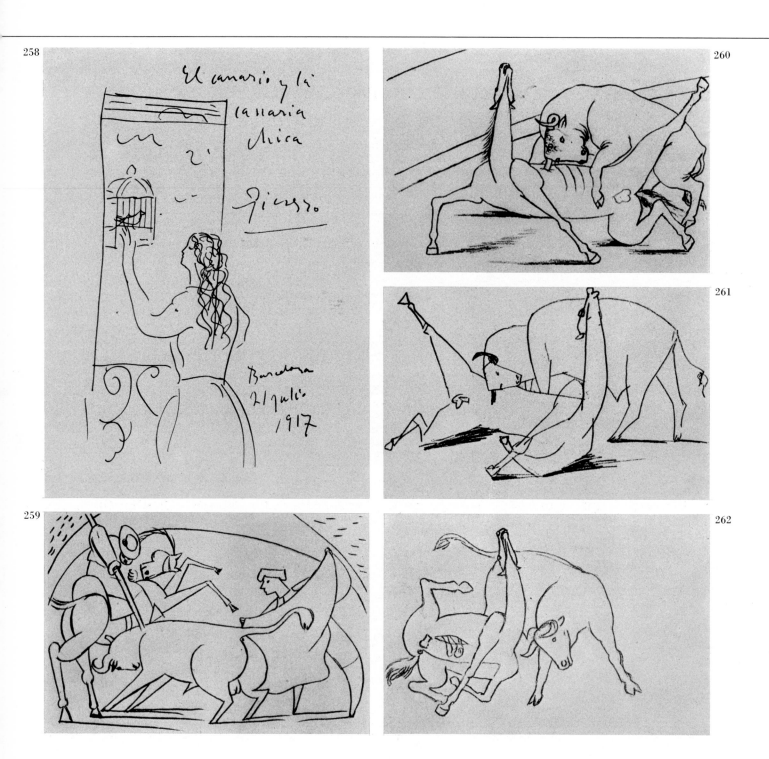

The conductor was Ernest Ansermet, of whom Picasso painted, about this time, a portrait which shows him alive and as if of stone at the same time.

Parade was not included in any of these six performances; another work was given instead, one that the company had probably brought to flatter the Spanish public a little. This work was called *Meninas* (Ladies in waiting), and it was included in the programme on the last night, June 30th.

This ballet, *Meninas*, the subject of which is the famous picture by Velázquez, had music borrowed from Fauré, choreography by Massine and costumes by Josep Maria Sert. It was very badly received by the public and has never been heard of since.

At this stage we might be justified in pausing for a moment to consider to what extent those *Meninas*, seen in the wings and in their dressing — rooms, seen during rehearsals or making their entrances and exits on the stage, left some obscure mark in Picasso's subconscious, for exactly forty years later he was to make them dance again in the theatre of his art, endowing them with an agitated, swift-changing life. And among these *Meninas*

was Olga Koklova. Was the struggle or confrontation with Velázquez's great painting a purely pictorial one, or was it that Picasso, in his 1957 reclusion, was partially reliving an important step, and certain decisive moments, in his youth?

The Ballet Company left Barcelona to continue its tour, but Picasso stayed in the city all that summer, working very hard.

His work during this stay is of unique, exceptional character. Very often in Picasso's work we can see two or three apparently opposed or divergent tendencies at the same time, but at this period we can say that everything he did was of divergent character and pointed in a different direction from the other works.

Some of the pictures, like the *Character at table* or the *Fruit bowl*, represent a sort of simplified return to geometric Cubism. It should be pointed out, however, that each of the compositions which could at this time be called Cubist is of a specific character. In one of them large planes are predominant and there is a tendency to abstraction; another is an entirely abstract composition; and the *Fruit bowl*, perfectly recognizable, is stylized Cubism. The *View of Barcelona*, with the monu-

263

264

ment to Columbus in the background, is a mixture of Cubism and Impressionism. The half-length *Manola* is done in a *pointilliste* technique and the *Ballarina*, which is a portrait of Blanquita Suárez, is in a Cubist style in which we can already see the beginnings of elements in contradiction to that style, elements which were to attain to their full development in that other character, the one I once described as "Ubuesque", because it is like an interpretation of Jarry's character. This work, in which the blues are predominant, might be described as a forerunner of a tendency — what was called "Curvisme"

— that was not to appear for another fifteen years.

From this period, too, we have the very well-known portrait of *Olga with a mantilla*, in which the evident intention was to emphasize the contrast between her Spanish style of dress and her markedly Slav face.

It was during this stay that Picasso painted *The Harlequin* — possibly the most famous of all his harlequins — which evokes those of the Rose Period. The latter, however, were more ethereal, while this one is much more corporeal. The head and, especially, the rather massive hands

are of our everyday world, not all evanescent, like so many of the faces and hands he painted in 1905. This *Harlequin*, which is undoubtedly the finest work he produced in this period, was later presented by Picasso himself to the Museum of Modern Art of Barcelona. It now occupies a place of honour in the Picasso Museum.

During this stay Picasso attended several bullfights and did a series of twenty quite remarkable sketches, clean in line, among which there is one of a disembowelled horse which was to serve as his model for the expressionistic horses he did in 1923 — and the scheme of which we can find at an even later date, in the horse in *Guernica*.

These sketches, together with some drawings of Olga and of other models, were all done in a single album, measuring 15.5 × 23 centimetres.

Picasso was much feted. Witness to this is a photograph in the "Galeries Laietanes" taken during that summer. In it we see him with some of the most important Catalan painters, Xavier Nogués, Ricard Canals; Manuel Humbert, Aragay, etc., as well as the collector Plandiura and the eminent critic Miquel Utrillo. Sitting on Picasso's left is Iturrino, with whom he held his first exhibition in Paris, and on his right Gustavo de Maeztu, of whom Picasso made a pencil drawing at about this time. But sitting at his feet is his faithful friend Angel F. de Soto, who, as if in further testimony of his nickname, *Patas* (Paws), presents himself to the camera feet first.

I should also mention the "Picasso banquet", which was held at the celebrated restaurant Lyon d'Or and was attended by a great number of friends of his: Pallarès, the Reventós brothers, the Soto brothers, Riera, Junyer-Vidal, Aragay, Carles, etc.

During those months Picasso became, so to speak, a Barcelona citizen once more. He often went to lunch at the Canari de la Garriga, where he left evidence of his presence in the form of a couple of sketches dated 21st July. In one of them the lovesick Picasso depicts Cupid wearing spectacles, with the caption: "Alas, love, what forms you reduce us to!"

During this sojourn in Barcelona he was staying with his family at No. 3 in the Calle de la Merced, as he himself confirmed to me years later. His home was very near the Pension Ranzini, in the Paseo de Colón, where the Diaghilev dancers (among them, of course, Olga Koklova) were putting up, and he spent so much time there that it has even been written, mistakenly, that he himself was staying at the pension. Picasso drew Olga repeatedly, several times on the balcony of the Pension Ranzini. Two of these drawings, done on the same spot, are useful to us as evidence of the dual tendency of his art at that time (the need to express the same things in a totally figurative language and in a schematized language) and of the simultaneity of these two forms of expression.

On November 5th the Russian Ballet Company returned to the Liceo to give a second series of performances, which were prolonged until the 18th of that month, and during which they presented, along with some of their previous successes, Stravinsky's *Fire bird* and *Petrouchka*.

It was on November 10th that they presented, for one performance only, the ballet *Parade*, which was awaited with a certain impatience and curiosity.

It we are to judge by the commentaries in the press, which would provide us with a whole anthology of unconscious humour, we must agree that the work caused a mixture of puzzlement and disapproval in the stalls, and only in the gallery was it greeted with enthusiasm.

The two extreme notes, one negative and the other positive, were sounded by the dailies "La Vanguardia" and "El Poble Català".

In "La Vanguardia" of the 11th we can read the following lines, signed Fausto: "If *Parade* is intended to be a serious work, we must take it as a joke; if, on the other hand, it is intended as a joke, *carried to such extremes*, then it is a joke in very bad taste and an application should be made to France for the extradition of its author, who is Spanish".

In the same day's number of "El Diluvio", and in an article signed by Alard, we read: "This is a work in which the décor, the characters and the music are all Cubist. Just imagine, even the music attempts to cube!"

"La Publicidad", which was then published in Castilian, was the paper that paid most attention to the ballet, to which it devoted almost a whole page. But its comments, and more specifically those of *Joan Sacs* (a pen-name used by Feliu Elias), were not very forthcoming. The aesthetic position of this critic was quite antipodean to that of Picasso.

The review in "El Poble Català" ended with the following words: "... Señor Fausto has a perfect right to condemn *Parade*. But what he has no right to do is to use expressions in abominably bad taste such as the one in which he speaks of 'demanding the extradition of the author', when he is referring to the greatest painter Spain has produced since Goya; nor should he make things even more confused, as he does when he speaks of Cubism and Futurism indistinctly." This review was not signed. Might it perhaps have been written by Eugeni d'Ors?

It was on the occasion of this presentation of *Parade* in Barcelona that Joan Miró first met Picasso.

Màrius Verdaguer has also told me about conversations Picasso had with Catalan intellectuals to discuss a suggestion first put forward by Eugeni d'Ors for producing a ballet with choreography by Diaghilev, music by the composer Pahissa and décor by Picasso, on Catalan themes: the *Patum*, or Corpus Christi celebration at Berga, the human pyramids formed by the men called the *Xiquets* at Valls, etc.

In the 1918 almanac of "La Revista", at that time the review most respected by Catalan intellectuals, side by side with an enormous number of drawings by Catalan artists (Nonell, Canals, Nogués, Sunyer, Casanovas, etc.) there was a drawing by Picasso done in Barcelona in 1902, which at that time belonged to Domingo Carles.

How long did this second sojourn of Picasso's in Barcelona last? It is difficult to say with any exactitude. We know that the dancers of Diaghilev's company arrived from Madrid on 22nd June. But Picasso must have come to Barcelona before them, for on the 18th there is an article in "El Poble Català" about a suggestion for devoting a whole room to Picasso's work at the future Barcelona International Art Exhibition; a suggestion for which the artist had already expressed his gratitude, according to this article, and to further which he had promised to give all the facilities possible to him. Apart from this, the last reliable reference to Picasso that we have for this second 1917 stay is the mention made of his presence at the Canari de la Garriga on 21st July.

After the performances at the Liceo during the month of June, Diaghilev's company apparently set out on a tour of South America, and it was probably on this occasion that Olga Koklova decided to stay in Barcelona with Picasso. The painter Manuel Humbert told me that one of Picasso's greatest worries at this time was that of Olga's documents, because the Russian Revolution had made her temporary exile a permanent one. At Picasso's request Humbert himself, during one of his visits to Paris, went to see Jean Cocteau to ask him if he could manage to get the problem of Olga's passport solved. When the Diaghilev company returned to Barcelona in the month of November for their second season of performances there (and to present *Parade*), Picasso and Olga had very probably already left the city.

BARCELONA, 1926, 1933, 1934 (1936)

6. Barcelona, 1926, 1933, 1934 (1936). Picasso paid several visits to Barcelona subsequently to 1917, though of some of them there is no reliable evidence. I have, however, been able to find some details of those he made in 1926, 1933 and 1934.

It appears almost certain that he visited Barcelona in 1923, probably just before or after a visit to his friend Manolo at Ceret. But I have promised myself to refer here only to visits reliably recorded.

In the autumn of 1926, while the Galerías Dalmau were holding an exhibition which contrasted Catalan artists (Dalí, Mompou, Sunyer, Gausachs, Manolo, Humbert, Rebull, etc.) with certain French painters (Delaunay, Dufy, Laurencin, etc.) and others who were not French, Picasso was in Barcelona. He was staying at the Ritz and, in "La Publicitat" of October 19th, there appeared a *Conversation with Picasso*, signed A. F. (Angel Ferran), in which Picasso complained that people wanted to make him speak and, above all, to speak about painting, whereas his real trade was simply drawing and painting.

*   *   *

In 1933 Picasso arrived from Cannes in his big Hispano-Suiza, accompanied, as in 1926, by his wife, Olga, and their son Paulo, and with a little dog. He stayed at the Ritz, room 507. He arrived on August 18th and on the 22nd they went to spend the day in Sitges, which seems to have captivated him. But the news of his arrival seems to have spread rather late. "La Publicitat", one of the leading dailies, announced it on the 23rd, with a photo which was reproduced the next day in "La Humanitat". In "La Publicitat" an extensive article appeared, signed by Jaume Passarell, relating the journalist's visit to the Ritz, where he had seen the painter accompanied by Manolo, the Soto brothers, the Junyer-Vidal brothers, Picasso's nephews: Fin, Vilató...

The journalists were disappointed, for they had gone intending to interview him and get some declarations from him about painting. How little they knew Picasso! In the weekly "Mirador" of August 31st there was an article by E. F. Gual entitled: *Picasso won't talk.*

Picasso said that he had come for personal reasons and, above all, to see his mother.

He visited Montjuïc, most probably to see the grounds of the 1929 Exhibition and, especially, the park there, where he was astounded by the wonderful view of the city from this point. Picasso left Barcelona on the 25th or 26th of August.

*   *   *

A little over a year later Picasso passed through Barcelona again. This time he was nearing the end of a tour round the Peninsula: San Sebastian, Burgos, Madrid, the Escorial, Toledo, Saragossa and Barcelona, from which last he would return once more to Paris.

This time he reached Barcelona in the early days of September, but the newspapers said nothing about his arrival, except "La Publicitat", which published an article by its editor, Carles Capdevila, on the 6th; the article was entitled *Picasso in the Museum,* its principal subject being the visit the artist had paid to the Art Museum of Catalonia, accompanied by the then curator, Joaquim M. Folch i Torres, and other officials of the Museum, such as Vidal Ventosa, etc.

"Passing from one room to another, Picasso, confronted with those incomparable fragments of primitive Catalan art, admired their strength, their intensity and their craftsmanship; the sureness of vision and execution, the aplomb and conviction with which the hand of the unknown artist had expressed in those murals the ideas and feelings that filled his spirit; and he agreed unhesitatingly that our Romanesque Museum was something unique in the world, an essential document for all who wish to know the sources of western art, a priceless lesson for the moderns.

The Picasso we met the other day was a Picasso so approachable and cordial, so ready to remember old friendships, that the hours spent talking to him flew by without our noticing..."

This was the last visit Picasso ever paid to Barcelona.

We must remember that the unpleasant Calvet affair had just finished in Paris. In 1930 Miquel Calvet had bought from Picasso's mother, in Barcelona, 400 of Picasso's drawings and sketches for 1,500 pesetas, which he had later sold in Paris for 175,000 francs. Picasso sued him for breach of trust and the French courts delivered a strange, equivocal verdict.

In 1936 an important exhibition of works by Picasso was organized at the Sala Esteva by the group known as the ADLAN ("Amics de l'Art Nou", meaning "Friends of New Art"). It was several years since Picasso had had a one-man show in Catalonia. The reasons for this absence are diverse and complex, and this is not the place to go into them.

The ADLAN group, which Joan Prats had at first wanted to call the "Club of Snobs", brought to Barcelona twenty-five works by Picasso, all lent by collectors, from which they had eliminated — deliberately, according to their president, Josep-Lluís Sert — the Blue, Rose and Neoclassical Periods. The exhibition, therefore, constituted a kind of challenge. The organizers wanted to show those aspects of Picasso's work that were least in line with the established Barcelona ideas about the painter. This deliberate slanting in the choice of the works to be shown met with the response and repercussions that might have been expected and, though I myself am among those who like *all* of Picasso, since I regard his adventure in art as something unique and whole, I must agree that this exhibition served as a most efficacious testing agent. The show, however, did not have all the effect it might have, possibly because of the political fever then sweeping the country, which centred attention and passions on other fields. The opening took place on 13th January, at ten o'clock in the evening — a very unusual time. Also for the first time, at least at a one-man show, you had to pay to go in. Among the works shown there were three quite recent (1935) ones, some *papiers collés*, work from the dynamic Dinard period of 1928, etc.

This opening was held with some solemnity and was broadcast. Messages were read from Luis Fernández, Juli González and Salvador Dalí, who said, among other things, that the works shown were "a first-class express train which was arriving in Barcelona forty years late". Joan Miró spoke personally and, finally, Jaume Sabartés read some of Picasso's recent poems.

On the 17th, Paul Éluard, who had come expressly for the purpose, gave a lecture on Picasso in front of the paintings. The same day "La Publicitat" carried Éluard's portrait in pencil by Picasso, accompanied by a text by J. V. Foix: *An eight-day-old drawing by Picasso.*

The exhibition was well-attended, but the press, on the whole, inclined to be reticent or hostile. The critic of "Mirador" — the weekly paper of the élite — did not speak about it. Instead, the editor — in — chief, Just Cabot, wrote an article with a title which fairly summed up the prevailing opinion in Barcelona: *A disservice to Picasso.* On the other hand, in "La Publicitat" of the 15th, M. A. Cassanyes, taking advantage of the situation for his own purposes, declared that the work of Picasso was a great step forward in modern art, though he had not been able to arrive at the consequences of his own discoveries.

The exhibition closed on January 28th.

As though all this were not enough, the Summer 1936 number of the art review "D'Ací i d'Allà" carried an *Epistle to Picasso* by Eugeni d'Ors, the thesis of which was almost the exact opposite of the article by Cassanyes, and which served only to strengthen the reactionary attitude of many people in Barcelona and to increase the bewilderment of the public in general.

I have commented on this text at greater length in my book *Double essay on Picasso.*

PART THREE

In point of fact, his short visits to Barcelona in 1933 and 1934, and the visits, twenty years later (1953, 1954), to the Roussillon (Perpignan, Collioure, Ceret), were the last sojourns of Picasso in Catalan country. But it is curious to remark that the longer his physical absence, the greater grows his spiritual influence in Catalonia.

Shortly after these brief visits to Barcelona, on November 12th 1935, Picasso added to his entourage, as a kind of "confidential secretary", one of the Catalan friends of his youth: Jaume Sabartés. This relationship was to be an enduring one and, as we shall see, fruitful for Catalonia; it would take too long to set down here its various stages.

In the year 1938, Picasso presented the Museum of Barcelona with a copy of his great etching entitled *Minotauromachy*.

Among the many friends in Catalonia that Picasso kept all his life — apart from such close friends as Pallarès, Sabartés, Reventós, Vidal Ventosa, etc., whose friendship was lifelong and unwavering — we should make special mention of the group of Catalan sculptors. Really they do not form a group at all, but with each of them individually Picasso kept up a deep and lasting friendship: Manolo, Casanovas, Gargallo, González, Fenosa, Rebull...

But with none of them, perhaps, was the relationship so close as with Manolo, one of the friends with whom Picasso had most enjoyed himself in his Bohemian days. Friends in Barcelona, the friendship continued in Paris and Ceret and ended only with Manolo's death.

Perhaps we should add to this list the name of that great French Catalan sculptor whom Picasso met most of all at Ceret, and for whom he felt a profound admiration: Arístides Maillol.

The Catalan spirit of Picasso, though needing no demonstration — for many years he had a giant photograph of a Catalan peasant in his studio — was manifested once more in 1946, when he participated in the Exhibition of Catalan Art in Paris.

Catalan literature on Picasso had been, until recently, very scant. It consisted almost entirely of articles like those we have already mentioned, or like that by Llorenç Artigues in "La Gaseta de les Arts" (March, 1925), a number almost completely devoted to Picasso, the one by Rafael Benet in the first number of "Art" (October, 1933), or those by Sebastià Gasch in "Mirador", perhaps the most understanding... The first book written wholly about Picasso *by* a Catalan was that by Eugeni d'Ors, with the double paradox that it was written in Castilian and the first edition appeared in French (1930). In the year 1946 a book called *Picasso antes de Picasso* (Picasso before Picasso) was published, by another Catalan, Alexandre Cirici-Pellicer, also written in Castilian. But in the spring of that same year the author of the present work wrote the first book on Picasso in Catalan, a book which, for obvious reasons, though Ferran Canyameres had announced its publication in a collection for 1947, was to remain unpublished for sixteen years. Only some chapters of it were sporadically published.

Ferran Canyameres, who had been one of the prime movers in the Exhibition of Catalan Art in Paris, and who was on friendly terms with Picasso, obtained the latter's consent to the publication, in 1947, of *Two stories (The centaur picador* and *Twilight of a faun)* by Ramon Reventós (1882-1923), illustrated by four dry-points by Picasso. The painter, who admired intensely the humour of this prematurely dead friend of his youth, had harboured this idea for some time. During the spring of 1947 the moment was propitious, for it coincided with the irruption into his work (white period of Antibes) of all those mythological creatures (centaurs, nymphs, fauns), brothers to those of Reventós. Picasso himself has told me that in order to illustrate these stories properly he copied out the whole Catalan text by hand, and thus the first series of illustrations has that air of a swiftly piercing wound which goes so well with the lightning-fast irony of Ramon Reventós. Of this book a printing of two hundred and fifty copies was made. For the French edition Picasso did four more plates.

Just before Christmas 1948, and for the first time in many years, an exhibition of works by Picasso opened in Barcelona. It was in the Galeries Laietanes and consisted of sixteen works of the 1901-1904 period and twenty-six lithographs dating from 1946-47.

Picasso wearing a *barretina* (typical Catalan peasant's cap).

266. Catalan wearing the traditional Catalan cap, the *barretina* (with a dedication to Joan Rebull). Paris, 24th June 1944. Pen and ink, 32 × 25 cm. Joan Rebull Collection, Barcelona.

266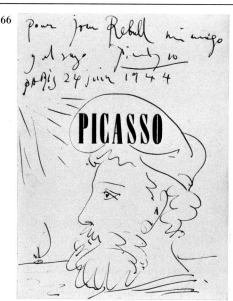

Picasso spent the three months of the summer of 1953 in the house of the Comte de Lazerme, in Perpignan, from which he made several excursions round the Roussillon countryside, drawing the beach and harbour of Collioure and also doing a long series of quick sketches, in a sure and vigorous line, of faces from the district.

During this stay the most important visits were those to Ceret during the months of August and September. On the first of these they organized a luncheon and a trip to Fontfreda, a peak from which one can see the whole of the Ampurdán (the north-western part of Spanish Catalonia) and the bay of Rosas

267. Illustration for *El centaure picador*, by Ramon Reventós. Paris, 1947. Dry-point.

268. Illustration for *El centaure picador*, by Ramon Reventós. Paris, 1947. Dry-point.

267

268

269. Illustration for *El capvespre d'un faune*, by Ramon Reventós. Paris, 1947.
Dry-point.
270. Illustration for *El capvespre d'un faune*, by Ramon Reventós. Paris, 1947.
Dry-point.

270

226

on one side and, on the other, the Roussillon and the Mediterranean, almost as far as Sète. In the course of this luncheon Señor Sageloli suggested to Picasso the idea of erecting a monument to bullfighters in Fontfreda, which would be a place of pilgrimage. Picasso seized upon Señor Sageloli's idea, but said it would be better to build a temple of Peace, for which he even drew a sketch. Looking out over that immense landscape, Picasso exclaimed: "Why should there be a frontier here? Here it is all the same land, the same people, the same language..."

As is well-known, this was the period of his first disagreements with Françoise Gilot, but it was also here that one could first feel the presence of Jacqueline, of whom he made several drawings before she knew it herself. The woods of Fontfreda were the first to witness their relationship.

The following year he again spent the summer in Perpignan, and once more made excursions around the Roussillon. The project of the monument at Fontfreda was not forgotten, but was always put off.

During these visits, as on those shorter ones in later years, he was often accompanied by Jean Cocteau, and it was almost always to preside over some festival or bullfight.

On November 10th 1955, a group of Catalans, including Jaume Sabartés, Joan Vidal Ventosa, Antoni Clavé, Miquel and Joan Gaspar and the latter's wife, Elvira, visited Picasso at his house in Cannes. Picasso himself, most unusually for him, went to meet them at the station that morning. He had not seen his friend Vidal Ventosa for over twenty years, and it was mainly in the latter's honour that he made this exception. From this moment on Picasso's relations with Barcelona became frequent and regular once more. An uninterrupted series of exhibitions, with the most diversified works, began to be held, from the following year, in the Sala Gaspar. The first, containing thirty-nine lithographs, took place between the 6th and the 19th of October 1956; the second, one of great variety, in order to give Barcelona a sample of Picasso's multiple activities (painting, sculpture, drawing, ceramics, mosaics), lasted from October 30th to November 29th of 1957.

Meanwhile, during the month of January of 1956, Picasso had been visited by

271. Portrait of Rosita. 1954. Conté pencil and charcoal on paper, 65 × 50 cm. Rosa Hugué Collection, Caldes de Montbui (Barcelona).

272. A centaur with a *porrón*. With a dedication to Dr Jacinto Reventós of the book by his brother Ramon. Paris, 28th April 1949. Lead pencil. Dr Jacinto Reventós Collection, Barcelona.

273. Mme de Lazerme in Catalan costume. 18th August 1954. Pen and ink on paper (unpublished).

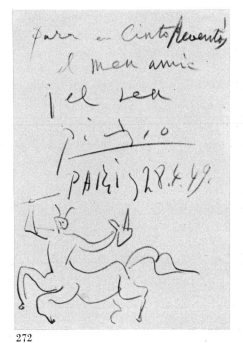

272

273

Gustau Gili and his wife, Ana María, whose object was to continue the initiative of Gili's father, founder of "Ediciones La Cometa", who in 1927, inspired by Agustí Calvet (Gaziel), has asked Picasso to illustrate the Tauromaquia (Art of bullfighting) of Pepe Illo.

In the spring of the following year, according to David Douglas Duncan, Picasso created in three hours the twenty-six marvellous aquatints which illustrate the text of Pepe Illo, and which record consecutively the whole course of a bullfight. The book, which came out in an edition of two hundred and fifty copies, in a format of 35 by 49 centimetres, was considered the bibliophile's masterpiece of the year 1959.

In 1957 Picasso made a donation of sixteen splendid ceramics to the city of Barcelona. These ceramics were intended for the Ceramic Museum of the city.

In April 1958, as if sent miraculously to join in this renewal of Catalan enthusiasm for Picasso, there appeared in Paris the facsimile edition of the sketchbook he had carried with him all the time he was in Gósol in 1906, under the title of *Catalan Sketchbook*, edited by Douglas Cooper.

During 1959 the "Cercle Artístic de Sant Lluc" (a Barcelona art association and school) organized an auction of works by Catalan painters, given by the artists, to raise funds: Picasso was the first of all, with a magnificent pastel in full colour, representing a monkey-painter, which can now be seen in the Picasso Museum.

But all of this seems a mere preamble to two projects on a larger scale, which were to set the seal on Picasso's relations with Barcelona: I refer to the friezes for the Architects' Association and to the Picasso Museum.

The first of these is due to the initiative of the architect Xavier Busquets, who had won the competition for a design for the

274

275

276. Scene from *La Tauromaquia*. (Drawing dedicated to Mauricio Torra-Balari in a copy of *La Tauromaquia*.) Mougins, 6th January 1960. India ink. Page measuring 35 × 49.5 cm. M. Torra-Balari Collection, Barcelona.

LA TAUROMAQUIA

a

b

new seat of the Catalonia and Balearics Architects' Association, in Barcelona, and who found himself faced with the problem of covering vast mural spaces, inside and outside. Xavier Busquets informed Picasso, by all the means at his disposal, of the siting and shape of the building, and Picasso, on October 15th of 1960, drew the cartoons — on scales of 1 : 10 and 1 : 5 — for carrying out these enormous friezes, the actual execution of which, by means of sand jets on blocks of concrete, was entrusted to the Norwegian artist Carl Nesjar. In these friezes, identifying himself once more with the country of his youth, Picasso describes, in an idiom at once simple and masterly, some of the most popular scenes of Catalan folklore: the "Giant" and "Giantess" of the processions, the "Xiquets" of Valls already

c

mentioned, etc. Xavier Busquets has told me that, when he explained all these things to the painter with the help of a 16 mm. film, Picasso remembered them all perfectly. One of the interior murals represents a vast "Sardana" (the Catalan round dance), embracing the whole of Catalonia, from the Pyrenees, on the peaks of which the theme of the four bars (of the Catalan flag) are repeated, right down to the sea...

The theme of the Sardana was to be repeated several times in those years, from the one he dedicated to Father Escarré, the Abbot of Montserrat, to those done on linoleum, in yellow and red to evoke the colours of the Catalan flag, for an exhibition of his work in Ceret in 1958, or for "Sardana Day" at Llançà on April 29th 1962.

That same year saw the apparition — on "Book Day", which is celebrated in Catalonia on April 23rd, St George's day — of *Vides de Picasso* (Lives of Picasso), by the author of the present work, which was really the first on Picasso to be written in Catalan. It is true that Sr. Joan B. Cendrós, for Christmas of 1960, had sent his bibliophile friends an opuscule entitled *Picasso, traductor de Maragall*

277. Poster by Picasso announcing his exhibition at the Sala Gaspar, Barcelona, in April 1961. Lithograph in five colours, 72 × 52 cm.

278. The *porrrón*. Postcard. Cannes, 16th November 1956. Coloured pencil, 15 × 22 cm. Sala Gaspar, Barcelona.

277

279. Poster by Picasso announcing his exhibition at the Sala Gaspar, Barcelona, in November-December 1960. Lithograph, 90 × 65 cm.

280. Poster by Picasso announcing his exhibition at the Sala Gaspar, Barcelona, in April 1961. Lithograph, 90 × 65 cm.

281. Poster by Picasso announcing his exhibition at the Sala Gaspar, Barcelona, in January-February 1961. Lithograph not used, since this exhibition was not held. 76 × 56 cm.

282. Poster by Picasso announcing his exhibition at the Sala Gaspar, Barcelona, in March 1968. Lithograph, 76 × 56 cm.

278

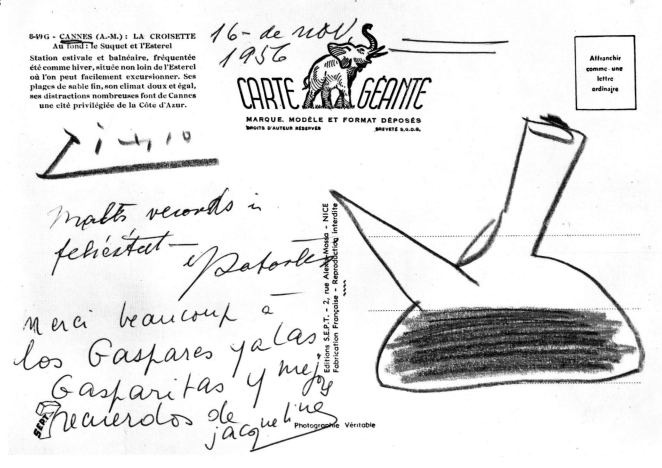

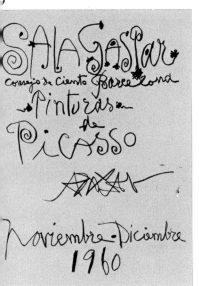

280

281

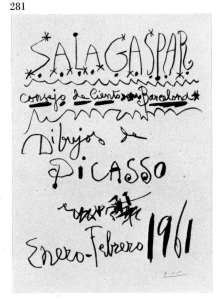

282

283. Poster by Picasso announcing his exhibition in Ceret, from 15th Juillet to 15th October 1958.

Picasso with Josep Palau i Fabre.

284. La sardana. Mougins, 2nd July 1959. Lithograph. This copy dedicated to the Abbot of Montserrat, 26th January 1961. Monastery of Montserrat, Barcelona.

283

285. Picasso with Pallarès, photographed by David Douglas Duncan and transformed by Picasso into Roman senators. Mougins, 5th October 1960. Coloured pencil on photograph, 34×27 cm. Private collection. Barcelona.

286. The monkey painter. Mougins, 2nd May 1959. Coloured pencil, 29×37 cm. Picasso Museum, Barcelona.

285

286

2 de
mayo
1959

238

a and b) Two aspects of the exterior of the Architectural Association of Barcelona,
     with the sgraffiti by Picasso.

a

b

(Picasso, translator of Maragall), in an edition of two hundred and twenty-five copies, in which he discussed at length the book of Ramon Reventós, the *Catalan Sketchbook* and the *Tauromaquia*.

Evoking Barcelona once more, through one of her most typical characters, Picasso gave new life, in some lithographs done on June 21st and July 6th, to "Senyor Esteve", the celebrated Barcelona character created by Santiago Rusiñol.

In the autumm of 1962 the terrible floods of the Vallés district, which cost so many lives and wreaked so much havoc, had international repercussions. Picasso, with his usual promptness, especially in the case of human suffering, made a most generous gesture, which did not, unfortunately, find its just reponse in Barcelona.

His example, however, was inmediately followed by other eminent artists, such as Miró, Braque, Chagall, Tàpies, Dalí, Clavé, Cuixart, etc. This is neither the time nor the place to recall our collective withdrawal. It is enough to remember that Picasso's gesture, in the end, was a donation of three million seven hundred thousand pesetas for the victims.

On December 24th of 1957 Picasso filled a little sketchbook with free evo-cations of the *Tauromaquia* of Pepe Illo, which he dedicated to Gustavo Gili; the latter published it in facsimile in 1963, and it is a real little gem for any biblio-phile.

In December 1963, too, the *Double essay on Picasso*, also written by the author of the present work, was awarded the Yxart Prize for essays and was published the following March.

After twenty-five years working for Picasso, Jaume Sabartés had accumulated a good collection of the master's works. Sabartés, who wanted to leave his treasures to a museum, decided, after consulting Picasso, and on the latter's recommendation, to give the whole to the City of Barcelona, on the express condition that a museum should be created to house it. The proposal came before the City Council, under the presidency of the Mayor, señor Porcioles, and was favourably received.

The City Council of Barcelona offered Jaume Sabartés the choice between two buildings and he decided on the Palace of Berenguer de Aguilar, built between the thirteenth and fifteenth centuries, in the "Calle Moncada". The works of restoration and installation were carried out

a

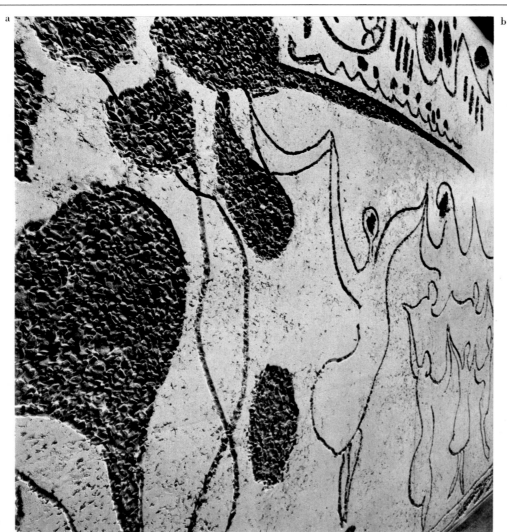

b

with excellent judgment, directed by the architect Joaquim Ros de Ramis and supervised by Joan Ainaud, Curator General of the Museums of Barcelona. It is almost impossible here not to mention that during the execution of these works some magnificent Gothic paintings of secular subject matter were discovered. The Palace of Berenguer de Aguilar, con-

taining the Sabartés donation — which includes the entirety of Picasso's lithographic work — was opened on March 9th of 1963. Soon, however, it was enriched by the greater part of works by Picasso which the city already possessed in the Museum of Modern Art, including the works from the Plandiura collection, acquired by the "Generalitat" (the

autonomous Catalan government) in 1933, and the works by Picasso which formed part of the Lluís Garriga Roig legacy. Some private donations, such as that made by Domènec Carles of his portrait by Picasso, those of Gala and Dalí, she with a *collage* and he with a print of the *Metamorphosis*, those of the brothers Gaspar or that of Gustau Gili, who donated the cancelled plates of the *Tauromaquia*, have since come to enrich the original nucleus, and all together form our splendid Picasso Museum, the pride of Barcelona, linking our city forever to the greatest artist of our time.

But all of these events have since had an unexpected, and even overwhelming, sequel. I refer to the donations subse-

a) Interior courtyard of the Palace of Berenguer de Aguilar, now the Picasso
    Museum

b, c, d, e and f) Various interior views of the Picasso Museum, Barcelona.

a

b

c

d

e

f

a, b, c, d, e, f and g) Other views of the Picasso Museum, Barcelona.

a

b

c

d

e

f

g

a, b, c and d)   Details of the Picasso Museum, Barcelona.

quently made by Picasso to the museum that bears his name in Barcelona. After the death of Sabartés (13th February 1968), Picasso gave the museum, in memory of his friend, the whole series of *Las Meninas* (58 oil paintings), along with the portrait he did of Sabartés in Paris towards the end of 1901. And two years later (23rd February 1970), he made a formal donation, in the presence of the Barcelona notary Noguera de Guzmán, of everything he had kept for many years in his family's home in Barcelona. With this donation the Picasso Museum of Barcelona, since enlarged by the acquisition of the adjoining mansion of the Baron de Castellet, has become an inestimably rich collection and certainly an unrivalled place for studying the works of the artist's youth.

c

d

287. Still life "La Desserte". Paris, 1901. Oil on canvas, 59 × 78 cm. Picasso Museum, Barcelona.

288. La Nana. Paris, autumn 1901. Oil on cardboard, 102 × 60 cm. Picasso Museum, Barcelona.

287

289. Sebastià Junyer-Vidal. Barcelona or Paris, 1903 or 1904. Oil on paper, 56 × 16 cm. Picasso Museum, Barcelona.
290. **Portrait of Señora Canals.** Paris, 1904. Oil on canvas, 88 × 68 cm. Picasso Museum, Barcelona.

289

291. Wine-glass and packet of cigarettes. Paris, 1924. Oil on canvas, 16 × 22 cm. Picasso Museum, Barcelona.

292. Still life with glass, lemon and orange (?). Paris, 6th August 1943. Oil on canvas, 16 × 24 cm. Picasso Museum, Barcelona.

293. Flower piece. Paris, 22nd April 1943. Gouache on paper, 65 × 49.5 cm. Picasso Museum, Barcelona.

294. Portrait of D. Carles. Paris, 1921. Drawing in pencil, 31.5 × 22.5 cm. Picasso Museum, Barcelona.

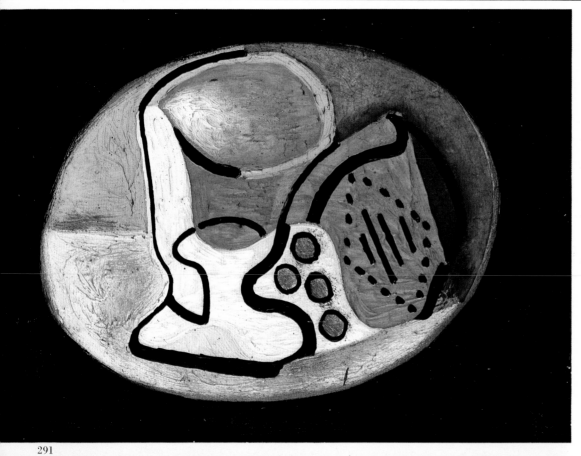

291

292

294

295. Jaume Sabartés. Royan, 22nd October 1939. Oil on canvas, 45.7×38 cm.
Picasso Museum, Barcelona.

295

296. Las Meninas (ensemble), No. 1. Cannes, 17th August 1957. Oil on canvas,
194 × 260 cm. Picasso Museum, Barcelona.

297. Las Meninas (the Infanta Margarita María), No. 17. Cannes, 6th September 1957. Oil on canvas, 46 × 37.5 cm. Picasso Museum, Barcelona.

297

298. Las Meninas (María Agustina Sarmiento), No. 3. Cannes, 20th August 1957.
Oil on canvas. 46 × 37.5 cm. Picasso Museum, Barcelona.

298

299. Las Meninas (the Infanta Margarita María), No. 8. Cannes, 27th August 1957. Oil on canvas, 33 × 24 cm. Picasso Museum, Barcelona.

300. Las Meninas (the Infanta Margarita María), No. 9. Cannes, 27th August 1957. Oil on canvas, 33 × 24 cm. Picasso Museum, Barcelona.

301. Las Meninas (the Infanta Margarita María), No. 10. Cannes, 28th August 1957. Oil on canvas, 18 × 14 cm. Picasso Museum, Barcelona.

302. Las Meninas (the Infanta Margarita María), No. 11. Cannes, 28th August 1957. Oil on canvas, 18 × 14 cm. Picasso Museum, Barcelona.

303. Portrait of Jacqueline No. 57. Cannes, 3rd December 1957. Oil on canvas, 116 × 89 cm. Picasso Museum, Barcelona.

304. Painter at work. Mougins, 31st March 1965. Oil on canvas, 100 × 81 cm. Picasso Museum, Barcelona.

299

301

300

302

304

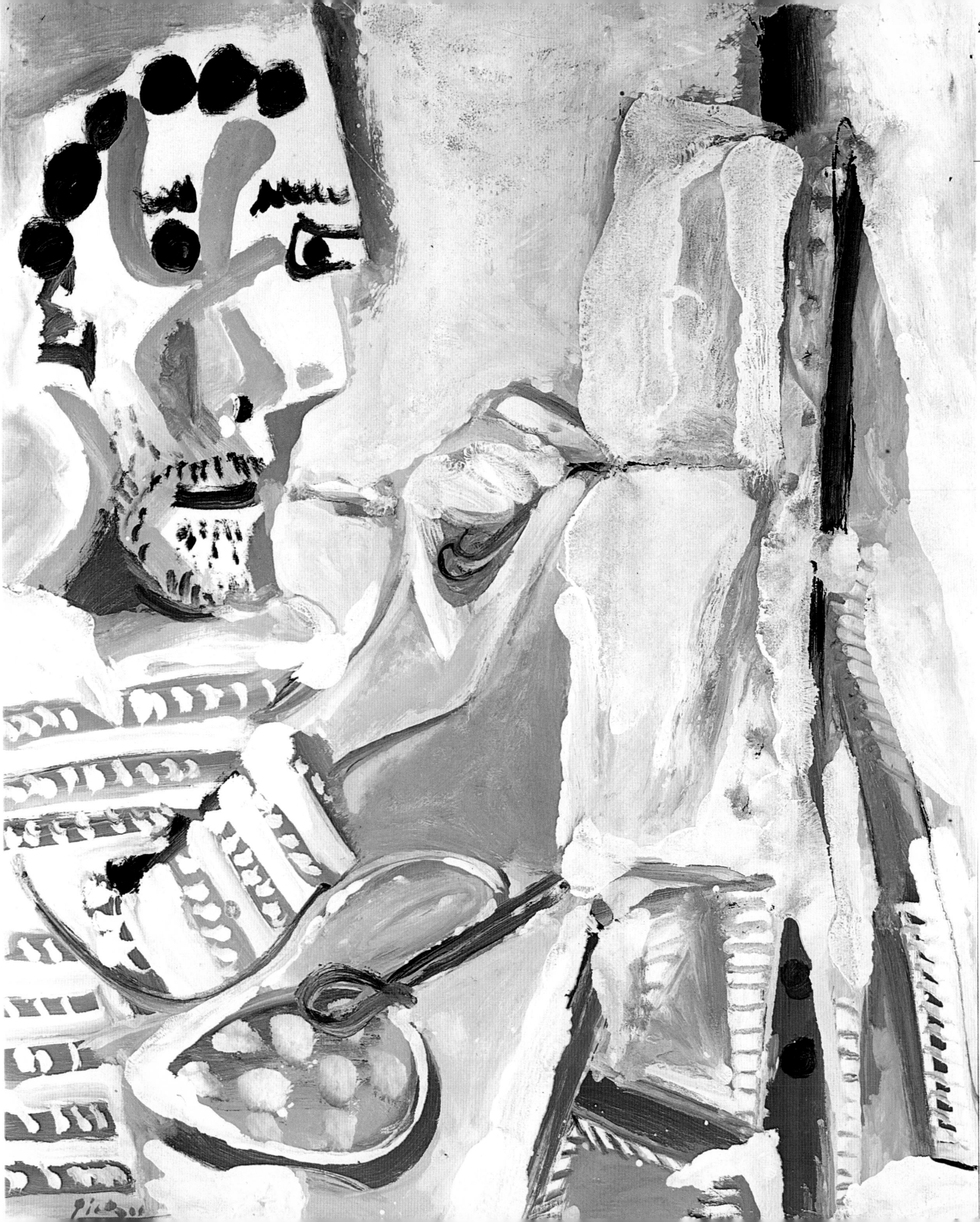

305. Barcelona, far away and vague in memory. Mougins, 30th September 1964.
Flomaster drawing, 9 × 21 cm. Sala Gaspar Collection, Barcelona.

306. Collage of the Catalan flag, executed on 11th July 1959 (on a lithograph dated
21st April 1958) and sent to the Gaspars, 14.5 × 10.5 cm. Sala Gaspar,
Barcelona.

305

306

APPENDIX

PICASSO AND HIS WORK

Pablo Ruiz Picasso! Here is a name which for many is practically unknown; for it should be properly understood that even most of those who "know" him do not know him sufficiently well to understand him or to judge him.

Picasso is still young, a mere stripling, but his work comes from remote places; it is ancient and it is modern: from an ancient world it has the impelling power that gives each work the finality of the idea of Art, while it is modern in its insatiable longing for novelty which destroys outworn prejudices and prevails over the old trends, that survive with the brittle rigidity of glass.

I declare, as I have said before, that to judge Picasso it is necessary to have a proper understanding of all men whose work in art is important and represents a sign of moral greatness in the development of the human spirit.

Picasso is more, infinitely more than many — even among those who seem to know him — believe. He is the beginning of an end. And by that I do not mean that his art is embryonic. On the contrary, through all his multiple evolutions he has traced a path that is straight, sure and precisely defined. He is the beginning of an end, not exactly because of any work in isolation, but because of the whole of which that work is a part, because of the way in which life is lived and felt by this artist — who, after all, is young, so that his work must necessarily be young too, but never premature. This, as a matter of fact, is the fundamental condition that tells us what Picasso is at the moment and what he will be in time to come. He is young, and because he is young he feels a penetrating perception, a mixture of depth, vision and "white-hot" poetry: that rectitude of spirit combined with the fire of the heart which is so admirably defined in those two beautiful lines:

Droit comme un rayon de lumière,
et comme lui vibrant et chaud.

For these reasons the work of Picasso has charm and a wonderful fascination. It is the aspect of power, of gaiety or sadness, of serenity, of easy elegance, which shows itself in each of his works in a way that is so free, so right for expressing the most powerful lamentations, the most subtle of dreams, the most intimate of songs and a "whole" that betokens a serious soul which in its perceptions, in its solitary agitations, has glimpses of an "infinite" and a "beyond".

In his insatiable urge to investigate, to scrutinize and to discover, this profound and purified perception that can be found in his work causes him to take his guessing beyond the visible. Form is the object and the medium; it is not subordinated to physiognomy, to expression, to gestures, to situations, or even to action. His work is pictorial and — at the same time and perhaps to a greater degree — artistically and intensely philosophical. He possesses the supreme Art — which in that is transcendental philosophy — of living, of feeling, of expressing...

In this sense Picasso triumphs: the conception of his very figures expresses it all. They are admirably drawn and they have a supreme stability that depends neither on the line nor on any more or less defined correctness. Almost all his figures, indeed, could be fused in gold work and in sculpture; his hands have touched the relief of the muscles, have followed the curve of the lines and felt the form of the bones. That is what is presented to us at first sight: the natural human figure, endowed with all the natural attitudes.

If, knowing him well, one considers how well he understands Art, Beauty, Love, Morals, if one observes the natural, impelling evolutions taking place in him, if one is familiar with his habits and his way of feeling life, then one can see an infinity of emanations and, shining in their midst, the same sort of imagination and spirit as breathes in his work.

And that is why we see him, taking the harmony of form as his starting-point and from that developing his powers, inflexible and penetrating. And because of that — and, perhaps, in spite of it — he pays less attention to externals than to content, preferring inner life to outer decoration; he is "religious" rather than idolatrous, "philosophical" rather than "picturesque", beautiful and splendid rather than pretty and flattering.

In his determination never to compromise with exigencies of any sort — not even with those that may come from his own inclinations — he never conceives what cannot delight himself before anybody else. That is why he eschews ordered accidents, the eruption of spontaneous, unconscious forces; and that is also why we have never seen him, in all his evolutions, exposed to the ultimate danger, that danger very few succeed in escaping: trivialism, the absolute negation of the idea of Art.

Picasso has always maintained his powers; he has always known how to develop, bringing his seeds to their flowering by new courses, without ever descending to trivialism.

His figures, which to some peoply may have seemed to be in full strength today, in depression tomorrow, have always been strong. In each and every one of the objects he depicts there is a foundation of throbbing beauty and truth, qualities that have always saved him from any sort of deviation, error or atavism. The object acquires strength, not only because it is in accord with the idea, but because it responds absolutely to the ideal, clearly expounded and defined.

The same subjects chosen by him could be interpreted in one way, or in exactly the opposite way, or in any of the ways in between the two, and they would always have the same strength, the same fascination, the same charm.

Obviously, since artists are so different in talent, inventiveness, culture and education, they are affected in different ways by one and the same object; each of them forms an original idea of it and this idea, made manifest in the artist's new output, suddenly installs a new work in the gallery of ideal forms.

But it is also obvious that the work that is most deeply impressed, the one that is most beautifully conceived, the one that best responds to the aim dictated by the ideal of Art, will be the one that achieves the greatest significance when it meets the test of experimental reality.

There are plenty of examples. Plautus, for the theatre of his day, conceived Euclion, the poor miser; then Molière took the same character and created Harpagon, the rich miser. Another two centuries elapse and we meet old Grandet; no longer silly and grotesque, as in the earlier works, but terrible and triumphant; and the same miser, taken from his provincial background and transformed into a Parisian, a cosmopolitan and drawing-room poet, appears again in the form of the usurer Gobseck, yet another creation of Balzac.

What all this amounts to is that Picasso's "work" has in some way the force of the works of some of those great men whom their posterity has pronounced immortal. He has been able to drink from those springs and has thus formed his personality, as his "work" indicates quite clearly. The objects he describes give an outer form (as occurred with the ancients) to the consequences of the psychological temperament, with all the varieties of the bilious, lymphatic, nervous or sanguine temperament.

But all of this is identified, not in fact by external details, but by the psychological tension of cases and things...

The effect of this impact is a strong and persuasive emotion; it is the link, the direct connection established by the artist's vision in this ascendancy of voluntary impression.

You may adorn this with beautiful names; you may call it inspiration, genius, feeling. But if you want to be precise in your definition, you will always have to record the vivid sensation that groups around it all the entourage of the ideas, the perceptions, the feelings and, in short, the whole metamorphosis it uses in order to reveal itself.

It is not a question of looking at this painting or that drawing, at this or that subject. You must contemplate the whole ensemble, the "total *œuvre*", and see the road he has gone.

Picasso is one of the few spirits in Spain who have collaborated in the work of faith.

His artistic temperament — free, strong, impulsive, recognizing no school and submitting to no conventional procedures, not fitting into any mould or accepting this or that dogma, refusing to admit any authority or to bow low before any idol — always tends to adorn itself in the vitality of thought, in the supreme power of the spirit. That is why we see, over and over again, that his vision is frank and strong, bold and audacious: loving, human, just and always questing after the sublime ideal of Beauty.

Each new production of this young artist is a step further that leads the beginning to the end; it is a sample of the higher life, the ascending life; for Picasso is not one of those who merely detest imbecility, routine, indifference — negative phases in the social consciousness — without succeeding in replacing them with new affirmations. Quite the contrary, in fact; he works with faith, enthusiasm and tenacity, deepening his convictions with each passing day, and his forces explode, collide and mark the end of the day's work.

There are very few indeed who possess honesty like his in Art. His skill is really frightening, and if he wanted to he could produce a lot and live well on the procéeds. But he sacrifices himself in this sense, refusing to gratify the frenchified public. How stupid these embryonic fools are who regard Art as a craft or pastime that anybody can engage in.

Let it be understood that Picasso's work must not be compared with anything that is produced in this country. It is something else; bear that in mind, you intelligent laymen!

Picasso is returning to Paris in a very few days. There, at least, he can be properly judged and discussed.

Carlos Juñer-Vidal

"El Liberal", 24th March 1904.

INDEX OF WORKS

56. Lady sitting at a table in the "4 Gats". Barcelona, 1899. Lead pencil.

57. Interior of the "4 Gats". The man at the table represents the poet Nogueras-Oller. Barcelona, 1899. Oil, 41×28 cm. Simon M. Jaglom Collection, New York.

58. Jaume Sabartés as a "decadent poet". Barcelona, 1900. Charcoal and water-colour on paper, 48×32 cm. Picasso Museum, Barcelona.

59. Jaume Sabartés. Barcelona, 1900. Charcoal and water-colour on paper, 50.5×33 cm. Picasso Museum, Barcelona.

60. Ricard Opisso. Barcelona, 1900. Drawing with coloured background, 31×22 cm. J. A. Samaranch Collection, Barcelona.

61. Joaquim Mir. Barcelona, 1899. Coloured drawing.

62. Pujolà i Vallés. Barcelona, 1899. Coloured drawing.

63. Carles Casagemas. Barcelona, 1899. Coloured drawing.

64. Santiago Rusiñol. Barcelona, 1899. Coloured drawing.

65. Picasso (self-portrait). Barcelona, 1899. Coloured drawing.

66. Pere Romeu. Barcelona, 1899. Coloured drawing.

67. Juli Vallmitjana. Barcelona, 1899. Coloured drawing.

68. Ramon Pitxot. Barcelona, 1899. Coloured drawing.

69. Soler. Barcelona, 1899. Coloured drawing.

70. Ramon Casas. Barcelona, 1899. Coloured drawing.

71. H. Anglada Camarasa. Barcelona, 1899. Coloured drawing.

72. Manolo Hugué. Barcelona, 1900.

73. Joan Gay. Barcelona, 1900.

74. H. Anglada Camarasa. Barcelona, 1900.

75. The composer Morera. Barcelona, 1900. Charcoal drawing, 18×13 cm. Jordi Gimferrer Collection, Banyoles (Gerona).

76. Ramon Pitxot. Barcelona, 1900.

77. Josep M. Folch i Torres. Barcelona, 1900.

78. J. Vallhonrat. Barcelona, 1900.

79. J. Vidal Ventosa. Barcelona, 1900. Charcoal drawing with brown-coloured background. According to Vidal Ventosa, this background was obtained by dipping the brush into a cup containing coffee grounds mixed with water. 47×27.5 cm. Picasso Museum, Barcelona.

80. Cinto Reventós. Barcelona, 1900. Charcoal drawing, 42×34 cm. Dr Cinto Reventós Collection, Barcelona.

81. The tailor Soler. Barcelona, 1900.

82. Angel F. de Soto (unpublished).

83. Josep Rocarol. Barcelona, 1900.

84. Mateu F. de Soto. Barcelona, 1900.

85. Joan B. Fonte. Barcelona, 1900. Charcoal drawing, 52×32.7 cm. Fogg Art Museum, Harvard University, Cambridge, Massachusetts.

86. Angel F. de Soto. Barcelona, 1900. Charcoal drawing, 43×24 cm. Autograph of Picasso, on the back of a photograph of the drawing, recognizing it as his own work.

87. Drawing done by Picasso in 1898, which appeared in the Almanac of the "Esquella de la Torratxa" for the year 1899.

88. Illustration for *To be or not to be*, by J. Oliva Bridgman, published in the magazine "Joventut" on 16th August 1900, Barcelona.

89. Illustration for *The virgins' clamour*, by J. Oliva Bridgman, published in the magazine "Joventut" on 12th July 1900. Barcelona.

90. Illustration for the short story *The madwoman*, by Surinyac Senties, published in the review "Catalunya Artística" on 6th September 1900. Barcelona.

91. Carles Casagemas, full-face and in profile. Barcelona, 1900. Drawing, 13×21 cm. J. A. Samaranch Collection, Barcelona.

92. Fita y Fita, Picasso's pupil. Barcelona, 1900.

93. Antoni Busquets i Punset, a prizewinner at the Floral Games. Drawing published in the review "Catalunya Artística" on 6th September 1900. Lead pencil and charcoal on paper, 17.5×12.7 cm. Private collection, Barcelona.

94. Bullfight. 1900. Oil on canvas, 47×56 cm. Galerie Georges Petit, Paris.

95. Bullfight. Barcelona, 1901. Charcoal and pastel, 15×22 cm. Private collection, Barcelona (unpublished).

96. Bullfight. 1900. Gouache, 16.2×30.5 cm. Cau Ferrat Museum, Sitges (Barcelona).

97. Bullfight. 1901. Oil on canvas, 53×68 cm. Niarchos Collection.

98. Pere Manyac, Picasso's first dealer. Paris, 1901. Oil on canvas, 100.5×67.5 cm. National Gallery of Art (Chester Dale Collection), Washington, D. C.

99. Jaume Sabartés, one of the last works painted by Picasso in Paris in 1901 or early in 1902. Oil on canvas, 46×38 cm. Picasso Museum, Barcelona.

100. Pen-and-ink drawing, accompanying a poem by P. Prat Jabal·lí published by the review "Auba" in its April 1902 number (unpublished document).

101. The "4 Gats" circle, with Picasso in the foreground, Pere Romeu on his left and, behind him, Rocarol, Fontbona, Angel F. de Soto and Jaume Sabartés, standing. Barcelona, 1902. Pen and ink, 31×34 cm.

102. Card announcing the birth of Pere and Corina Romeu's son. Barcelona, 12th May 1902. Postcard, 9×14 cm. Private collection, Barcelona.

103. Postcard advertising "Lecitina Agell". Barcelona, 1902. Postcard, 9×14 cm. J. Palau i Fabre Collection, Barcelona.

104. The dead woman. Barcelona, 1902-1903. Oil on canvas, 44.5×34.1 cm. Picasso-Reventós Foundation, Barcelona.

105. Portrait of S. Junyer-Vidal by Picasso, reproduced in "El Liberal" on 16th October 1902, on the occasion of an exhibition by the former (unpublished document).

106. The blue houses. Barcelona, 1902. Oil, 50.5×40.5 cm.

107. Front page of the daily newspaper "El Liberal" on 5th October 1902, evoking the traditional Barcelona festivities of Our Lady of Ransom. Barcelona.

108. Drunk woman drowsing (or "The absinthe drinker"). Barcelona, 1902. Oil on canvas, 80×62 cm. Dr Huber Collection, Glarus (Switzerland).

109. Woman squatting. Barcelona, 1902. Oil on canvas, 63.5×50 cm. Carl Bertel Collection, Nathorst, Stockholm.

110. Seated woman. Picasso's first sculpture. Barcelona, 1902. Replica in bronze, 15×11.5×8.5 cm. Picasso Museum, Barcelona.

111. The woman with a chignon. Barcelona, 1902. Oil on canvas, 100×69 cm. Formerly in the Paul Guillaume Collection, Paris.

112. Nude from behind. Barcelona, 1902. Oil on canvas, 46×40 cm. Private collection, Paris.

113. The woman with the shawl. Barcelona, 1902. Oil on canvas, 65×54 cm. Galerie Georges Petit, Paris.

114. Mother and children on the seashore. Barcelona, 1903. Pastel, 46×31 cm.

115. Portrait of Corina Jáuregui, Pere Romeu's wife. Barcelona, 1902. Oil on canvas, 60×48 cm. Formerly in the Picasso Collection.

116. Cocottes in the bar. Barcelona, 1902. Oil on canvas, 80×91.5 cm. M. Walter P. Chrysler Jr Collection, New York.

117. Poor people on the seashore. Barcelona, 1903. Oil on wooden panel, 105.4×69 cm. Chester Dale Collection, National Gallery of Art, Washington.

118. The housetops of Barcelona. Barcelona, 1903. Oil on canvas, 71×112 cm. Formerly in the Picasso Collection.

119. Barcelona nocturne, from the studio in the Riera de Sant Joan. Barcelona, 1903. 54×45.5 cm. E. G. Bührl Family Collection, Zürich.

120. The offering. 1902. Drawing in India ink, 25×26 cm. Mr and Mrs Sidney Elliot Cahn Collection, New York.

121. The soup. Barcelona, 1902 or 1903. Oil on canvas, 37×45 cm. J. H. Crang Collection, Toronto, Canada.

122. The unkempt' girl. Barcelona, 1903. Water-colour on paper, 50×37 cm. (In this picture, as in others of the same period, the colouring material used may have been a sort of Reckitt's blue, a cheap product which Picasso used and mixed with other materials in preparing his colours.) Picasso Museum, Barcelona.

123. "Forsaken". Barcelona, 1903. Pastel and charcoal on paper, 46×40 cm. Picasso Museum, Barcelona.

124. Mother and child in profile (Maternity on the seashore). Barcelona, 1902 or 1903. Oil on canvas, 83×60 cm. Galerie Beyeler, Basel.

125. Poor couple with child. Barcelona, 1903. Blue pencil, 13.5×9 cm. Private collection, Barcelona.

126. Sketch for the picture "Couple in a café". Barcelona, 1903. Coloured pencils, 13.5×9 cm. Private collection, Barcelona.

127. Couple in a café. Barcelona, April 1903. Oil on canvas, 81.5×65.5 cm. Nasjonalgalleriet, Oslo.

128. The blind singer. Barcelona, 1903. Bronze, 13×7×8 cm.

129. Blue portrait of Angel F. de Soto. Barcelona, 1903. Oil on canvas, 69.7×55.2 cm. Mr Donald Stralem Collection, New York (unpublished in colour).

130. The embrace. Barcelona, 1903. Pen-and-ink drawing. Vidal de Llobatera Collection, Barcelona.

131. The embrace (or "La joie pure"). Barcelona, 1903. Pastel, 98×57 cm. Musée de l'Orangerie Jean Walter-Paul Guillaume Collection, Paris.

132. Sketch for "Life". Barcelona, 1903. Pen and ink, 15×11 cm.

133. Sketch for "Life". Barcelona, 1903. Drawing in pen-and-ink and pencil, 27×20 cm. Roland Penrose Collection, London.

134. Life. Barcelona, 1903. Oil on canvas, 197×127.3 cm. The Cleveland Museum of Art (Hanna Fund donation), Cleveland, Ohio.

135. The old Jew. Barcelona, 1903. Oil on canvas, 125×92 cm. Pushkin Museum of Fine Arts, Moscow.

136. Page of drawings, with sketch for "The old Jew". 1902. India ink, 38×46 cm.

137. Sketch for the "Head of a Picador". Barcelona, 1903. Conté pencil, 14.5×14 cm.

138. Head of a Picador. Barcelona, 1903. Bronze, 18.5×11 cm.

139. The old guitarist. Barcelona, 1903. Oil on wood, 121×82 cm. The Art Institute of Chicago.

140. Sebastià Junyer-Vidal with a woman beside him. Barcelona, June 1903. Oil on canvas, 125.5×91.5 cm. Mrs David Edward Bright Collection, Los Angeles.

141. The blind man. Barcelona, 1903. Oil on canvas, 95.24×94.61 cm. Metropolitan Museum of Art (Mr and Mrs Ira Hampt donation, 1950), New York.

142. Portrait of Señora Soler. Barcelona, 1903. Oil on canvas, 100×70 cm. Bayerischen Staatsgemäldesammlungen, Munich.

143. The Soler family. Barcelona, 1903. Oil on canvas, 150×200 cm. Musée des Beaux-Arts, Liège.

144. The tailor Soler. Barcelona, 1903. Oil on canvas, 100×70 cm. Hermitage Museum, Leningrad.

145. Christ. Barcelona, 1902. Drawing in lead pencil, 37×26.7 cm., according to Zervos.

146. The tailor Soler. Barcelona, 1903. India ink with colour wash, 22×16 cm.

147. Self-portrait in profile. Barcelona, 1903.

148. Woman's head. Barcelona, 1903. Pen-and-ink drawing.

149. Evocation of Horta de Ebro. Barcelona, 1903.

150. Shepherd with his flock. Evocation of Horta de Ebro. Barcelona, 1903. Charcoal and pencil on Ingres paper, 47.7×59 cm. Rudolphe Staechelin Foundation, Basel.

151. Old woman in Sunday best. Evocation of a character in Horta de Ebro. Barcelona, 1903.

152. Family scene. Evocation of Horta de Ebro. Barcelona, 1903. Pen-and-ink drawing with colour wash, 31.5×43 cm. Albright-Knox Art Gallery, Buffalo, New York.

153. The poor man's meal. 1903. Water-colour, 24×33 cm. Galerie Beyeler, Basel.

154. Sebastià Junyer-Vidal with a lyre. Barcelona, 1903. Coloured drawing, 36×25.5 cm.

155. Sebastià Junyer-Vidal dressed as a bullfighter. Barcelona, 1903. Pen-and-ink drawing with colouring, 13.5×9 cm. Private collection, Barcelona.

156. Sebastià Junyer-Vidal, the painter. Barcelona, 1903. Pen-and-ink drawing with colouring, 13.5×9 cm. Private collection, Barcelona.

157. The madman. Barcelona, 1904. Water-colour on wrapping paper, 85×35 cm. Picasso Museum, Barcelona.

158. The poor people. Autumn 1903. Blue drawing in pencil, 46.8×36 cm. Heydt Museum, Wuppertal-Elberfeld, Germany.

159. Head of bearded man, apparently a preparatory sketch for "The madman". Barcelona, 1904. Drawing, 30×21 cm., according to Zervos.

160. Poor wretches. Barcelona, autumn 1903. Pen and ink with blue wash, 37.5×27 cm. Whitworth Art Gallery, University of Manchester.

161. The Palacio de Bellas Artes of Barcelona. Barcelona, autumn 1903. Oil on canvas, 60×40 cm. Private collection (unpublished in colour).

162. Self-portrait of Picasso painting "La Celestina". Barcelona, 1903 or 1904. Drawing in Conté pencil and colour.

163. Sketch for "La Celestina", with S. Junyer-Vidal and a young woman. Barcelona, 1904. Coloured pencils, 27×23.5 cm.

164. Picasso with S. Junyer-Vidal and a "Celestina" in a tavern. Barcelona, 1903-1904. Pastel, 26×33 cm.

165. La Celestina. Barcelona, 1904. Oil on canvas, 81×60 cm. Max Pellequer Collection, Paris. (Ektachrome "Editions Cercle d'Art", Paris.)

166. Portrait of Jaume Sabartés. Barcelona, spring 1904. Oil, 49.5×38 cm. Kunsternes Museum, Oslo.

167. Portrait of Lluís Vilaró. Barcelona, 1904. Oil on wood, 45×24.5 cm.

168. Picasso leaving for Paris with Junyer-Vidal. Barcelona, April 1904. Drawing in pen-and-ink and coloured pencils, 22×16 cm. Picasso Museum, Barcelona.

169. Landscape of Gósol. Summer 1906. Painting.

170. Sketch from the *Catalan Sketchbook*, representing a peasant woman of Gósol. Gósol, summer 1906. Drawing, 11.5×7 cm.

171. Sketch from the *Catalan Sketchbook*. Summer 1906. This sketch seems to have been done looking at the outline of the village which can be seen from the inn known as Can Tempanada. Pencil, 11.5×7 cm.

172. Self-portrait of Picasso, shortly after his arrival in Gósol. 1906. Charcoal.

173. Swineherd guarding a herd of pigs. 1906. Pencil and India ink, 21×20 cm. Galerie Louise Leiris, Paris.

174. A group of pigs. 1906. Pencil and India ink, 21.5×27.5 cm. Galerie Louise Leiris, Paris.

175. Scene in the interior of Can Tempanada. Gósol, 1906. Conté pencil, 16.5×22 cm.

176. The two brothers. Gósol, spring 1906. Gouache on cardboard, 80.3 × 60.2 cm. Formerly in the Picasso Collection.

177. Sketch for "The two brothers". Gósol, 1906. Pen and ink, 29 × 21.5 cm. Dr Warner Muenstesberger Collection, New York.

178. Sketch for "The two brothers". Gósol, 1906. Drawing in India Ink, 31 × 23.5 cm. The Baltimore Museum of Art (the Fine Foundation).

179. The harem ("Figures in pink"). Gósol, summer 1906. Oil, 154 × 110 cm. The Cleveland Museum of Art (Leonard C. Hanna Jr Collection), Cleveland, Ohio.

180. "La toilette". Gósol, summer 1906. Oil on canvas, 151 × 90 cm. Albright-Knox Art Gallery, Buffalo, New York.

181. Adolescents. Gósol, summer 1906. Oil on canvas, 157 × 117 cm. Formerly in the Paul Guillaume Collection, intended for the Orangerie des Tuileries, Paris.

182. Double page from the *Catalan Sketchbook*, with a sketch for 'The three Graces' on one side and the copy of a poem by Maragall on the other. Gósol, summer 1906. The pages measure 11.5 × 7 cm.

183. The two adolescents. Gósol, 1906. Oil on canvas, 151.5 × 93.7 cm. Chester Dale Collection, National Gallery of Art, Washington.

184. Donkey's head and dog curled up. Gósol, 1906. Wash drawing, 17 × 11 cm. Kirchheimer Kusmacht Collection, Zürich.

185. Woman on a donkey, with the Pedraforca mountain in the background. Gósol, 1906. Wash drawing, 17 × 11 cm. Kirchheimer Kusmacht Collection, Zürich.

186. Fernande Olivier in Gósol peasant costume, with the Pedraforca in the background. Gósol, 1906. Oil on wood, 81.5 × 62 cm.

187. Still life with *porrón*. Gósol, 1906. Oil on canvas, 38.5 × 56 cm. Hermitage Museum, Leningrad.

188. Still life with pictures in the background. Gósol, 1905. Oil on canvas, 82 × 90 cm.

189. *Porrón*, jug and grapes. Gósol, 1906. Water-colour, 34 × 38 cm.

190. Nude with her hands clasped (Fernande Olivier). Gósol, 1906. Gouache on canvas, 96.5 × 75.6 cm. Art Gallery of Ontario, Canada.

191. Bust of woman, full-face. Gósol, 1906. Pen and ink, 17 × 10.5 cm.

192. The Andorran women. Gósol, summer 1906. Pen and ink, 59 × 35 cm. Art Institute of Chicago, Chicago.

193. Couple on a feast-day. 1906. Pen and ink, 21 × 12.5 cm.

194. Bust of woman in semi-profile. Gósol, 1906. Pencil and gouache.

195. Woman's head. Gósol, 1906. Pen and ink.

196. Woman's head in semi-profile. Gósol, 1906. Pen and ink, 21 × 13.5 cm.

197. Woman wearing a kerchief on her head. Gósol, 1906. Gouache on paper, 66 × 49.5 cm. T. Catesby Jones Collection, Virginia Museum of Fine Arts, Richmond, Virginia.

198. Young man from Gósol with his cap pushed back. Gouache, 61.5 × 58 cm. Göteborgs Kunstmuseum, Göteborg, Sweden.

199. The woman with the loaves. Gósol, summer 1906. Oil, 100 × 73 cm. Philadelphia Museum of Art (Charles E. Ingersoll donation), Fairmount, Philadelphia.

200. Three nudes. Gósol, summer 1906. Gouache, 62 × 47 cm. Max Pellequer Collection, Paris.

201. Stylized head of Josep Fontdevila. Gósol, 1906. Water-colour.

202. Hairdressing. Paris or Gósol, 1906. Oil on canvas, 175 × 99.7 cm. Metropolitan Museum of Art, New York (Wolfe Fund).

203. Three heads. Horta de Ebro, summer 1909. Oil on canvas, later divided into two. According to Zervos, the head on the left measures 35.5 × 32 cm., while those on the right measure 35.5 × 35 cm. Walter P. Chrysler Jr Collection, New York.

204. Portrait. Horta de Ebro, summer 1909. Conté pencil, 47.5 × 23.2 cm.

205. Manuel Pallarès. Barcelona, 1909. Oil on canvas, 68.5 × 50.5 cm. Private collection, Barcelona.

206. The mountain of Santa Bárbara, near Horta de Ebro. Horta de Ebro, summer 1909. Oil on canvas, 65 × 54 cm. Formerly in the A. Vollard Collection, Paris.

207. The factory at Horta de Ebro. Horta de Ebro, summer 1909. Water-colour. Formerly in the A. Flochtheim Collection.

208. The oil mill. Summer 1909. Pen and ink, 32 × 17 cm.

209. Sketch for "The reservoir at Horta". Horta de Ebro, summer 1909. Pen and ink, 11.3 × 14.4 cm.

210. Sketch for "The reservoir at Horta". Horta de Ebro, summer 1909. Pen and ink, 20.3 × 13 cm.

211. The reservoir at Horta. Horta de Ebro, summer 1909. Oil on canvas, 81 × 65 cm. Private collection, Paris.

212. Houses in Horta de Ebro. 1909. Oil on canvas, 38 × 46 cm. R. Dutilleul Collection, Paris.

213. Houses on the hill. Horta de Ebro, summer 1909. Oil on canvas, 65 × 81 cm. Formerly in the Gertrude Stein Collection, Paris.

214. The factory at Horta de Ebro. Horta de Ebro, summer 1909. Oil on canvas, 53 × 60 cm. Hermitage Museum, Leningrad.

215. Nude in an armchair. Horta de Ebro, summer 1909. Oil on canvas, 92 × 73 cmm. Douglas Cooper Collection, London.

216. Woman with a bunch of flowers beside her. Horta de Ebro, summer 1909. Oil on canvas, 61 × 50 cm. Wright Ludington Collection.

217. Woman's head with mantilla. Horta de Ebro, summer 1909. Oil on canvas, 39 × 30 cm. R. Dutilleul Collection, Paris.

218. Woman's head. Horta de Ebro, summer 1909. Oil on canvas, 65 × 54 cm. Formerly in the Paul Guillaume Collection, Paris.

219. Head of Fernande. Horta de Ebro, summer 1909. Oil on canvas, 61 × 42 cm. Kunstsammlung Nordrhein-Westfalen, Düsseldorf.

220. Woman's head. Horta de Ebro, summer 1909. Oil on canvas, 61 × 50 cm. Formerly in the A. Vollard Collection, Paris.

221. The bottle of Anís del Mono. Horta de Ebro, summer 1909. Oil on canvas, 81 × 55 cm. Walter P. Chrysler Jr Collection, New York.

222. Front page for "Arte Joven", second period (1st September 1909). (Unpublished document.)

223. The guitarist. Cadaqués, summer 1910. Oil on canvas, 100 × 73 cm. Musée National d'Art Moderne, Paris.

224. Glass and lemon. Cadaqués, summer 1910. Oil on canvas, 100 × 73 cm. William Averell Harriman Collection, New York.

225. Woman with mandoline. Cadaqués, summer 1910. Oil on canvas. Formerly in the A. Vollard Collection, Paris.

226. "Mademoiselle Léonie on a chaise-longue". Cadaqués, summer 1910. Etching to illustrate Max Jacob's *Saint Matorel* (Plate III), 18.8 × 14.2 cm.

227. Nude woman. Cadaqués, summer 1910. Oil on canvas, 118 × 61 cm. Mme Mérie Callery Collection, Paris.

228. The harbour of Cadaqués. Summer, 1910. Oil on canvas, 38 × 45.5 cm. Narodnigalerie, Prague. Provenance: V. Kramar Collection; acquired in 1960.

229. The fan. Ceret, summer 1911. Water-colour, 30 × 22 cm. J. Leperrier Collection, Paris.

230. The fan. Ceret, summer 1911. Oil on canvas, 61 × 50 cm. Formerly in the Paul Guillaume Collection, Paris.

231. Character with pipe. Ceret, summer 1911. Pencil drawing.

232. Landscape of Ceret. Ceret, summer 1911. Oil on canvas, 65 × 50 cm. Solomon R. Guggenheim Museum, New York.

233. The poet. Ceret, summer 1911. Oil on canvas, 130 × 89 cm. Peggy Guggenheim Foundation, Venice.

234. Fruit bowl and fruit. Ceret, summer 1912. Oil on canvas, 55 × 38 cm. Alphonse Kahn Collection.

235. The Spaniard. Ceret, spring 1912. Drawing and glued papers, 62.5 × 47 cm. P. Gaut Robinson Collection.

236. The accordeonist. Ceret, summer 1911. Oil on canvas, 130 × 89 cm. Solomon R. Guggenheim Museum, New York.

237. The bottle of Vieux Marc. Ceret, spring 1912. Drawing and glued papers, 63 × 49 cm. Musée National d'Art Moderne (Cuttloli-Laugier donation), Paris.

238. Violin. Ceret, 1912. Oil on canvas, 54.5 × 54 cm.

239. The violin ("Jolie Eva"). Ceret, spring 1912. Oil on canvas, 81 × 60 cm. Staatsgalerie, Stuttgart.

240. Fiestas in Ceret. Ceret, spring 1912. Oil on canvas, 24 × 41 cm. Mme P. Sacher Pratteln Collection, Basel.

241. Spanish still life. Ceret, spring 1912. Oil on canvas, 46 × 33 cm. R. Dutilleul Collection, Paris.

242. "Amics, cantem la ceretana". Ceret, 1912 or 1913. Pen-and-ink drawing (unpublished).

243. Girl's head. Ceret, spring 1913. Oil on canvas, 55 × 38 cm. Musée National d'Art Moderne (Cuttloli-Laugier donation), Paris.

244. Harlequin. Ceret, 1912. Oil on canvas, 88.5 × 46 cm. Haags Gemeentemuseum, The Hague.

245. Bottle of Vieux Marc. Ceret, 1912. Drawing and glued papers, 62.5 × 47 cm. Musée National d'Art Moderne, Paris.

246. Ceret, 1913. Glued papers, charcoal and pastel, 47.7 × 63 cm.

247. Olga seated on the balcony of the Pension Ranzini. Barcelona, 1917. Lead pencil, 23 × 15.5 cm.

248. Olga writing on the balcony of the Pension Ranzini. Barcelona, 1917. Lead pencil, 23 × 15.5 cm.

249. Olga, in profile. Barcelona, 1917. Lead pencil, 23 × 15.5 cm.

250. Olga wearing a Spanish mantilla. Barcelona, 1917. Oil on canvas. Formerly in the Picasso Collection.

251. Character. This seems to be an interpretation of Jarry's Ubu. Barcelona, 1917. Oil on canvas, 92 × 70 cm. Picasso Museum, Barcelona.

252. Character at table, in neo-Cubist manner. Barcelona, 1917. Oil on canvas, 100 × 71 cm. Picasso Museum, Barcelona.

253. Fruit bowl with fruit. Barcelona, 1917. Oil on canvas, 38 × 28 cm. Picasso Museum, Barcelona.

254. Manola, done with a *pointilliste* technique. Barcelona, 1917. Oil on canvas, 118 × 89 cm. Picasso Museum, Barcelona.

255. Blanquita Suárez. Barcelona, 1917. Oil on canvas, 108 × 60 cm. Picasso Museum, Barcelona.

256. Gonzalo de Maeztu. Barcelona, June 1917. Pencil drawing, 39 × 32 cm. Torelló Collection, Barcelona.

257. The balcony (Barcelona composition with the Columbus monument in the background.) Barcelona, 1917. Oil on canvas, 39 × 33 cm. Picasso Museum, Barcelona.

258. The cock canary and the little hen canary. Barcelona, 21st July 1917. Pen and ink on paper. Andreu Collection, Barcelona.

259. Bullfight. Barcelona, 1917. Lead pencil, 23 × 15.5 cm.

260. Bullfight. Barcelona, 1917. Lead pencil, 23 × 15.5 cm.

261. Bullfight. Barcelona, 1917. Lead pencil, 23 × 15.5 cm.

262. Bullfight. Barcelona, 1917. Lead pencil, 23 × 15.5 cm.

263. Portrait of Ernst Ansermet. Barcelona, 1917. Pencil on paper, 22.5 × 13 cm. Formerly in the Ernst Ansermet Collection, Switzerland.

264. Study for "Harlequin". Barcelona, 1917.

265. The Barcelona Harlequin. Barcelona, 1917. Oil on canvas, 116 × 90 cm. Picasso Museum, Barcelona.

266. Catalan wearing the traditional Catalan cap, the *barretina* (with a dedication to Joan Rebull). Paris, 24th June 1944. Pen and ink, 32 × 25 cm. Joan Rebull Collection, Barcelona.

267. Illustration for *El centaure picador*, by Ramon Reventós. Paris, 1947. Dry-point.

268. Illustration for *El centaure picador*, by Ramon Reventós. Paris, 1947. Dry-point.

269. Illustration for *El capvespre d'un faune*, by Ramon Reventós. Paris, 1947. Dry-point.

270. Illustration for *El capvespre d'un faune*, by Ramon Reventós. Paris, 1947. Dry-point.

271. Portrait of Rosita. 1954. Conté pencil and charcoal on paper, 65 × 50 cm. Rosa Hugué Collection, Caldes de Montbui (Barcelona).

272. A centaur with a *porrón*. With a dedication to Dr Jacinto Reventós of the book by his brother Ramon. Paris, 28th April 1949. Lead pencil. Dr Jacinto Reventós Collection, Barcelona.

273. Mme de Lazerme in Catalan costume. 18th August 1954. Pen and ink on paper (unpublished).

274. Aquatint from *La Tauromaquia*, by Pepe Illo. Cannes, spring 1957. Page measuring 35 × 49.5 cm.

275. Aquatint from *La Tauromaquia*, by Pepe Illo. Cannes, spring 1957, Page measuring 35 × 49.5 cm.

276. Scene from *La Tauromaquia*. (Drawing dedicated to Mauricio Torra-Balari in a copy of *La Tauromaquia*.) Mougins, 6th January 1960. India ink. Page measuring 35 × 49.5 cm. M. Torra-Balari Collection, Barcelona.

277. Poster by Picasso announcing his exhibition at the Sala Gaspar, Barcelona, in April 1961. Lithograph in five colours, 72 × 52 cm.

278. The *porrón*. Postcard. Cannes, 16th November 1956. Coloured pencil, 15 × 22 cm. Sala Gaspar, Barcelona.

279. Poster by Picasso announcing his exhibition at the Sala Gaspar, Barcelona, in November-December 1960. Lithograph, 90 × 65 cm.

280. Poster by Picasso announcing his exhibition at the Sala Gaspar, Barcelona, in April 1961. Lithograph, 90 × 65 cm.

281. Poster by Picasso announcing his exhibition at the Sala Gaspar, Barcelona, in January-February 1961. Lithograph not used, since this exhibition was not held. 76 × 56 cm.

282. Poster by Picasso announcing his exhibition at the Sala Gaspar, Barcelona, in March 1968. Lithograph, 76 × 56 cm.

283. Poster by Picasso announcing his exhibition in Ceret, from 15th July to 15th October 1958.

284. La sardana. Mougins, 2nd July 1959. Lithograph. This copy dedicated to the Abbot of Montserrat, 26th January 1961. Monastery of Montserrat, Barcelona.

285. Picasso with Pallarès, photographed by David Douglas Duncan and transformed by Picasso into Roman senators. Mougins, 5th October 1960. Coloured pencil on photograph, 34 × 27 cm. Private collection, Barcelona.

286. The monkey painter. Mougins, 2nd May 1959. Coloured pencil, 29 × 37 cm. Picasso Museum, Barcelona.

287. Still life "La Desserte". Paris, 1901. Oil on canvas, 59 × 78 cm. Picasso Museum, Barcelona.

288. La Nana. Paris, autumn 1901. Oil on cardboard, 102 × 60 cm. Picasso Museum, Barcelona.

289. Sebastià Junyer-Vidal. Barcelona or Paris, 1903 or 1904. Oil on paper, 56 × 46 cm. Picasso Museum, Barcelona.

290. Portrait of Señora Canals. Paris, 1904. Oil on canvas, 88 × 68 cm. Picasso Museum, Barcelona.

291. Wine-glass and packet of cigarettes. Paris, 1924. Oil on canvas, 16 × 22 cm. Picasso Museum, Barcelona.

292. Still life with glass, lemon and orange (?). Paris, 6th August 1943. Oil on canvas, 16 × 24 cm. Picasso Museum, Barcelona.

293. Flower piece. Paris, 22nd April 1943. Gouache on paper, 65 × 49.5 cm. Picasso Museum, Barcelona.

294. Portrait of D. Carles. Paris, 1921. Drawing in pencil, 31.5 × 22.5 cm. Picasso Museum, Barcelona.

295. Jaume Sabartés. Royan, 22nd October 1939. Oil on canvas, 45.7 × 38 cm. Picasso Museum, Barcelona.

296. Las Meninas (ensemble), No. 1. Cannes, 17th August 1957. Oil on canvas, 194 × 260 cm. Picasso Museum, Barcelona.

297. Las Meninas (the Infanta Margarita María), No. 17. Cannes, 6th September 1957. Oil on canvas, 46 × 37.5 cm. Picasso Museum, Barcelona.

298. Las Meninas (María Agustina Sarmiento), No. 3. Cannes, 20th August 1957. Oil on canvas, 46 × 37.5 cm. Picasso Museum, Barcelona.

299. Las Meninas (the Infanta Margarita María), No. 8. Cannes, 27th August 1957. Oil on canvas, 33 × 24 cm. Picasso Museum, Barcelona.

300. Las Meninas (the Infanta Margarita María), No. 9. Cannes, 27th August 1957. Oil on canvas, 33 × 24 cm. Picasso Museum, Barcelona.

301. Las Meninas (the Infanta Margarita María), No. 10. Cannes, 28th August 1957. Oil on canvas, 18 × 14 cm. Picasso Museum, Barcelona.

302. Las Meninas (the Infanta Margarita María), No. 11. Cannes, 28th August 1957. Oil on canvas, 18 × 14 cm. Picasso Museum, Barcelona.

303. Portrait of Jacqueline No. 57. Cannes, 3rd December 1957. Oil on canvas, 116 × 89 cm. Picasso Museum, Barcelona.

304. Painter at work. Mougins, 31st March 1965. Oil on canvas, 100 × 81 cm. Picasso Museum, Barcelona.

305. Barcelona, far away and vague in memory. Mougins, 30th September 1964. Flomaster drawing, 9 × 21 cm. Sala Gaspar Collection, Barcelona.

306. Collage of the Catalan flag, executed on 11th July 1959 (on a lithograph dated 21st April 1958) and sent to the Gaspars, 14.5 × 10.5 cm. Sala Gaspar, Barcelona.

PICASSO EXHIBITIONS IN BARCELONA

"4 Gats"	February 1900.
Sala Parés.	1-14 June 1901. Joint show with Ramon Casas, organized by "Pèl & Ploma".
Galerías Dalmau.	February 1912.
La Pinacoteca.	1-14 October 1932. This exhibition also included works by Ramon Casas. (I do not know whether it was actually held or not).
Sala Esteva.	13-28 January 1936. Organized by ADLAN.
Galerías Layetanas	24 December 1948 - 7 January 1949.
Sala Gaspar.	6-19 October 1956. 39 original lithographs.
Sala Gaspar.	30 October - 29 November 1957. Painting, sculpture, ceramics, mosaic.
Sala Gaspar.	July 1960. 45 linocuts.
Sala Gaspar	November-December 1960. 30 unpublished pictures.
Sala Gaspar.	April 1961. 72 drawings.
Syra.	3-15 November 1962. Three illustrated books.
Sala Gaspar.	24 November - 14 December 1962. 44 linocuts.
Sala Gaspar.	28 December 1963 - 24 January 1964. 25 linocuts.
Sala Gaspar.	15 July - 15 August 1965. Painting, tapestry, drawing, engraving.
Sala Gaspar.	January 1966. Graphic work.
Sala Gaspar.	March 1968. Painting, drawing, engraving.
Sala Gaspar.	11 December 1970 - 27 January 1971. 347 engravings.
Picasso Museum.	25 October 1971. Works by Picasso from the Hugué Collection.
Sala Gaspar.	25 October - End of November 1971. Painting, drawing.
Picasso Museum.	15 February - 14 March 1973. "Picasso and the Reventós family".
Sala Gaspar.	25 October - 7 December 1974. 67 water-colours, drawings and gouaches, from 1897 to 1971.

SELECT BIBLIOGRAPHY

GENERAL BIBLIOGRAPHY

BAS I GICH, JOAQUIM: *El carrer de Mont-sió, generador de les inquietuds artistiques barcelonines.* "Meridià". Barcelona, 20-V-1938.

BAS I GICH, JOAQUIM: *Pere Romeu, "cabaretier",* "Meridià". Barcelona, 5-VI-1938.

BAS I GICH, JOAQUIM: *Les classes de colorit i composició d'Antoni Caba.* "Meridià". Barcelona, 4-XI-1938.

BAS I GICH, JOAQUIM: *La personalitat múltiple d'Alexandre de Riquer,* "Meridià". Barcelona. 31-XII-1938.

BLADÉ DESUMVILA: *Carta oberta sobre Nogueres Oller.* "Serra d'Or", Montserrat, October 1962.

CABAÑAS GUEVARA, LUIS: *Cuarenta años de Barcelona, 1890-1930.* Ed. Memphis. Barcelona, 1944.

CARLES, D.: *Memorias de un pintor (1912-1930).* Ed. Barna. Barcelona, 1944.

CRASTRE, VÍCTOR: *Naissance du cubisme.* Ophrys (undated).

ELIES, FELIU: *L'escultura catalana moderna.* Ed. Barcino. Vol. I, Barcelona, 1926. Vol. II, Barcelona, 1928.

GALWEY, ENRIC: *El que he vist a can Parés en els darrers quaranta anys.* Sala Parés, Barcelona, 1934.

GARCÉS, TOMÀS: *Amb Nogueres Oller, del pamflet a l'idil·li.* "Serra d'Or". Montserrat, July 1962.

GASCH, SEBASTIÀ: *L'expansió de l'art català al món.* Barcelona, 1953.

GASCH, SEBASTIÁN: *Blanquita Suárez, "Cabecita a pájaros".* "Destino". Barcelona, 9-1-1971.

JARDÍ, ENRIC: *La ciutat de les bombes.* Dalmau, Barcelona, 1964.

JARDÍ, ENRIC: *Eugeni d'Ors. Vida i obra.* Aymà, S.A. Editora. Barcelona, 1967.

JUNOY, JOSÉ: *Arte y Artistas* (First series). Barcelona, 1912.

JUNOY, JOSEP M.: *El gris i el cadmi.* Llibreria Catalònia. Barcelona, 1926.

JUNOY, JOSEP M.: *L'actualitat artística.* Llibreria Catalònia. Barcelona, 1931.

MARÉS DEULOVOL, FEDERICO: *Dos siglos de enseñanza artística en el Principado.* Barcelona, 1964.

MARTINELL, CÉSAR: *La escuela de La Lonja en la vida artística barcelonesa.* Escuela de Artes y Oficios Artísticos. Barcelona, 1951.

MORENO, SALVADOR: *Interviu con Santos Torroella.* "El Noticiero Universal". Barcelona, 16-IX-1964.

ORS, EUGENI D': *Obra Catalana Completa. Glosari 1906-1910.* Ed. Selecta. Barcelona, 1950.

JUÑER VIDAL, CARLOS: *Picasso y su "obra".* "El Liberal". Barcelona, 24-III-1904.

QUATRE GATS: *Primer Saló "Revista".* Ed. Barna. Barcelona, 1954.

RÀFOLS, J.F.: *El arte modernista en Barcelona.* Dalmau. Barcelona, 1943.

RÀFOLS, J.F.: *Modernismo y Modernistas.* Ediciones Destino. Barcelona, 1949.

RÀFOLS, J.F.: *Diccionario biográfico de Artistas de Cataluña.* (3 volumes). Ed. Millà. Barcelona, 1951.

SALMÓN, ANDRÉ: *Souvenirs sans fin.* Vol. I. 1903-1908. Gallimard, 1955. Vol. II, 1908-1920, Gallimard, 1956.

SOLDEVILA, CARLOS: *El cincuentenario de 'El Guayaba'.* "Destino". Barcelona, 12-I-1952.

TORRES GARCÍA, J.: *Historia de mi vida.* Montevideo, 1939.

VERDAGUER, MARIO: *Medio siglo de vida íntima barcelonesa.* Ed. Barna. Barcelona, 1957.

VOLTES, PERE: Catalunya i la llibertat de comerç amb Amèrica. Dalmau. Barcelona, 1964.

VOLLARD, AMBROISE: *Souvenirs d'un marchand de Tableaux.* Albin Michel. Paris, 1959.

WEILL, BERTHE: *Pan! dans l'Œil!...* Librairie Lipschtz. Paris, 1933.

BIBLIOGRAPHY ESPECIALLY CONCERNING PICASSO

ALAVEDRA, JOAN: *Carner i Picasso.* "Tele-Estel". Barcelona, 26-V-1967.

ANON.: *L'Afer Picasso.* "Mirador". Barcelona, 5-IV-1934.

ANON. (Rodríguez Codolà): *Exposición Ruiz Picazzo* (sic). "La Vanguardia". Barcelona, 3-II-1900.

BARR, ALFRED H., Jr.: *Picasso. Fifty years of his art.* The Museum of Modern Art. New York, 1946.

BENET, RAFAEL: *Picasso i Barcelona.* "Art", No. 1, Barcelona, 1933.

BERNIER, ROSAMOND: *48 Paseo de Gracia,* "L'Œil", No. 4. 15-IV-1955.

BLUNT, ANTHONY & POOL, PHOEBE: *Picasso. The formative years.* Studio Books. London, 1962.

BRASSAÏ: *Conversations avec Picasso.* Gallimard. Paris, 1964.

CABOT, JUST: *Un mal servei a Picasso.* "Mirador". Barcelona, 23-I-1936.

CAPDEVILLA, CARLES: *Picasso al Museu.* "La Publicitat". Barcelona, 6-IX-1934.

CARNET CATALAN: Preface and notes by Douglas Cooper. Berggruen et Cie. Paris, 1958.

CARNET DE LA TAUROMAQUIA: Gustavo Gili and Professor Bernhard Geiser. "La Cometa". Barcelona, 1963.

CASSANYES, M.A.: *25 pintures de Picasso a Barcelona.* "La Publicitat". Barcelona, 14-I-1936.

CASSOU, JEAN: *Picasso.* Hyperion. Paris, 1940.

CENDRÓS, JOAN BAPTISTA: *Picasso, traductor de Maragall.* Barcelona, 1960.

CIRICI PELLICER, ALEXANDRE: *Picasso antes de Picasso.* Iberia. Joaquín Gil, publishers. Barcelona, 1946.

CIRICI PELLICER, ALEXANDRE: *Converses amb Picasso.* "Serra d'Or". Montserrat, February 1963.

COOPER, DOUGLAS: *Préface.* Picasso Exhibition. Musée Cantini. Marseilles, 1959.

COOPER, DOUGLAS: *Picasso y el teatro.* Spanish translation by Ana María Gili. Published by Ed. Gustavo Gili. Barcelona, 1968.

CÓRDOBA, MANUEL DE: *Los primeros dibujos que envió Picasso a Barcelona no se publicaron por malos.* "El Día Gráfico". Barcelona, 15-VI-1935.

DAIX, PIERRE: *Picasso.* Spanish translation by Gimeno Palmés. Revised and edited by Teodoro Miciano. Daimon. Madrid-Barcelona-México, 1965.

DAIX, PIERRE & BOUDAILLE, GEORGES: *Picasso 1900-1906.* Catalogue raisonné of the work in painting. Ed. Ides et Calendes. Neuchâtel, 1966.

DOUGLAS DUNCAN, DAVID: *El mundo privado de Pablo Picasso.* Spanish edition. Editorial Ridge Press. Novaro-México, S.A., 1958.

DOUGLAS DUNCAN, DAVID: *Los Picassos de Picasso.* Spanish translation by Juan Cortés. Ed. Rauter. Sala Gaspar Collection. Barcelona, 1961.

FERMIGIER, ANDRÉ: *Picasso.* Le Livre de Poche. Paris, 1969.

FOIX, J.V.: *Un dibuix de Picasso que té vuit dies.* "La Publicitat". Barcelona, 17-I-1936.

FOLCH Y TORRES, JOAQUÍN: *Picasso en Barcelona y el arte de Picasso.* "Destino". Barcelona, 31-VIII-1957.

GASCH, SEBASTIÀ: *Picasso.* "D'ací i d'allà". Barcelona, VI-1926.

GASCH, SEBASTIÀ: *Picasso i l'Impressionisme.* "Gaseta de les Arts". No. 44. Barcelona, 1-III-1926.

GASCH, SEBASTIÀ: *Picasso.* "Mirador". Barcelona, 22-V-1930.

GASCH, SEBASTIÀ: *Picasso, amb motiu d'una exposició.* "La Publicitat". Barcelona, 10-VIII-1932.

GASCH, SEBASTIÀ: *Unes declaracions de Picasso.* "Meridià". Barcelona, 27-V-1938.

GAZIEL (AGUSTÍ CALVET): *La naixença catalana de La Tauromàquia de Picasso.* Complete Works, pp. 1601-1604. Prologue by Josep Benet. Compilation, arrangement and notes by Tomàs Tebé. Ed. Selecta. Barcelona, 1970.

GIL DE BIEDMA, JAIME: *Monstruo en su laberinto.* "Don". No. 7. Barcelona, 1968.

JUÑER VIDAL, CARLOS: *Picasso y su "obra".* "El Liberal". Barcelona, 24-III-1904.

KAHNWEILER, DANIEL-HENRY: *Confessions esthétiques.* Gallimard. Paris, 1963.

LUJÁN, NESTOR: *Picasso y los toros.* "Destino". Barcelona, 6-II-1960.

LLORENS ARTIGAS, JOSEP: *Els grans mestres de la pintura moderna. Pau Ruiz Picasso.* "Gaseta de les Arts". No. 20. Barcelona, I-III-1925.

MORAGAS, RAFAEL: *Los famosos e inolvidables talleres que tuvo Picasso en Barcelona.* "El Día Gráfico". Barcelona, 12-XI-1938.

MORENO, SALVADOR: *Picasso, copista de museo.* "El Noticiero Universal". Barcelona, 23-VI-1971.

OLIVIER, FERNANDE: *Picasso et ses amis.* Ed. Stock. Paris, 1933.

ORS, EUGENIO D': *Pablo Picasso.* Editions des chroniques du jour. Paris, 1930.

ORS, EUGENI D': *Epístola a Picasso.* "D'ací i d'allà". Barcelona, summer 1936.

ORS, EUGENIO D': *Pablo Picasso en tres revisiones.* Ed. Aguilar. Madrid. Undated.

PASSARELL, JAUME: *Picasso a Barcelona.* "La Publicitat". Barcelona, 24-VIII-1933.

PENROSE, ROLAND: *Picasso, Vida y obra.* Spanish translation and notes by Concha G. de Marco., Published in Madrid, 1959.

PENROSE, ROLAND: *Portrait of Picasso.* The Museum of Modern Art, New York, 1957.

PERMANYER, LUIS: *Horas con Picasso.* "Destino". Barcelona, 22-VI-1963.

PERUCHO, JUAN: *Los dibujos de Picasso.* "El Arte en las Artes". Danae. Barcelona, 1965.

RÀFOLS, J.F.: *La etapa barcelonesa de Picasso.* "Destino". Barcelona, 3-III-1956.

RAYNAL, MAURICE: *Picasso.* Skira. Geneva, 1953.

RODA, PEDRO DE (Wenceslao F. de Soto): *La adolescencia barcelonesa del pintor Picasso.* "La Noche". Barcelona, 28-IX-1927.

RODRÍGUEZ CODOLÀ: See Anon. (2).

SABARTÉS, JAIME: *Picasso. Portraits et souvenirs.* Louis Carré et Maximilien Vox, publishers. Paris, 1946.

SABARTÉS, JAIME: *Picasso. Documents iconographiques.* Pierre Cailler. Geneva, 1954.

SABARTÉS, JAUME: *De Llotja al Museu Picasso. Les bleus de Barcelone.* Paris, 1963.

SACS, JOAN: *La pintura d'En Picasso.* (I & II). "Vell i Nou". Nos. 72 and 73. Barcelona, VIII-1918.

SACS, JOAN: *Miscel·lània d'art modern.* "La Publicitat". Barcelona, 8-IV-1936.

STEIN, GERTRUDE: *Autobiographie d'Alice B. Toklas.* French translation by Bernard Faid. Gallimard. Paris, 1934.

UTRILLO, MIQUEL (PINCELL): *Dibuixs d'en Picasso.* "Pèl & Ploma". Barcelona, VI-1901.

VALLENTIN, ANTONINA: *Picasso.* Albin Michel. Paris, 1957.

X.: *Picasso a Barcelona.* "El Matí". Barcelona, 25-VIII-1933.

ZERVOS, CHRISTIAN: *Pablo Picasso.* Volumes I to XXIV. Cahiers d'Art. Paris.

WRITINGS ON PICASSO BY THE PRESENT AUTHOR

Baudelaire-Picasso. "Ariel". Barcelona, XI-XII-1946.

Clima de miracle (Picasso as illustrator). "Ariel". Barcelona, VI-1947.

Goethe-Picasso. "Catalunya". Buenos Aires, 1947.

Faust-Picasso. "Ariel". Barcelona, I-1951. (Chapter from the book *Vides de Picasso*).

La vida (L'existència). End of 1960. Raixa. Palma de Mallorca, 1960. (Chapter fro the book *Vides de Picasso*).

El cubisme picassià. "Serra d'Or". Montserrat, VI-1961. (Chapter from the Book *Doble assaig sobre Picasso*).

Vides de Picasso (Assaig de biografía pura). Pedreira. Barcelona, 1962.

Doble assaig sobre Picasso. Awarded the Premi Yxart in 1963. Ed. Selecta, Barcelona, 1964.

Un capítol de la vida de Picasso a Catalunya. "El llibre de tohom", 1965, Alcides. Barcelona, 1965.

Picasso. "Biografies populars". Alcides-Aymà. Barcelona, 1965.

Picasso en Cataluña. (Text in four languages: Castilian, French, English, German). Ediciones Polígrafa. Barcelona, 1966.

Picasso a Catalunya. (Original Catalan text of the preceding work). Ediciones Polígrafa. Barcelona, 1967.

Doble ensayo sobre Picasso. (Castilian translation of *Doble assaig sobre Picasso*). With a special edition of 180 copies on linen paper, decorated with an original dry-point by Picasso and signed by the artist. G. Gili. Barcelona, 1968.

Les derniers dessins de Picasso. "Opus international". No. 7. Paris, VI-1968.

"Las Meninas" de Picasso. "Serra d'Or". Montserrat, XII-1968.

Picasso per Picasso. Joventut. Barcelona, 1970.

Picasso por Picasso. (Castilian translation of the preceding work). Juventud. Barcelona, 1970.

Picasso by Picasso. (German translation of the preceding work). Kolhammer. Stuttgart, 1970.

Las mocedades de Picasso en Barcelona. "La Vanguardia". Barcelona, 25-XII-1970.

Picasso i els seus amics catalans. Editorial Aedos. Barcelona, 1971.

Personas y personajes barceloneses del gran teatro del mundo de Picasso. "La Vanguardia". Barcelona, 24-X-1971.

1900 : un ami de jeunesse. Homage to Pablo Picasso. "XXᵉ siècle". Paris, 1971.

Le Musée Picasso de Barcelona. Homage to Pablo Picasso. "XXᵉ siècle". Paris, 1971.

L'extraordinària vida de Picasso. Ediciones Proa. Aymà. Barcelona, 1971.

La extraordinària vida de Picasso. (Castilian translation of the preceding work). Ediciones Proa. Aymà. Barcelona, 1972.

Homenatge a Picasso. Text —almost complete— of the entertainment preat "La Cova del Drac", Barcelona on 19 October 1971. Edicions 62. Barcelona, 1972.

Guernica n'est pas un tableau. Opus international. No. 38. Paris, XI-1972.

Una fuente que parecía inagotable. "La Vanguardia". Barcelona, 10-IV-1973.

Dol per Picasso. "Serra d'Or". Montserrat, V-1973.

La última juventud de Picasso. "La Vanguardia". Barcelona, 10-VI-1973.

Encara més sobre Picasso. (Interview with Palau i Fabre by Alex Broch). "Canigó", 23-VI-1973.

El Museo Picasso de Barcelona. "La Actualidad Española", 8-XI-1973.

La mort de Picasso. "Almanac de Serra d'Or". Montserrat, 1973.

The photographs reproduced in this book have been supplied by: Mme. Jacqueline Picasso, Català Roca, J. Palau i Fabre, Manuel Pallarès, Dr. Jacint Reventós, Sala Gaspar, J. Vidal-Ventosa and Archivo Mas, as also by the various museums in which the original works are hung. The photograph of Picasso on page 223 has been supplied by M. Raymond Fabre, of the Studio Visage, Perpignan.

The author has great pleasure in publicly expressing his gratitude for the assistance received on various occasions to Messrs. Manuel Pallarès, Joan Vidal-Ventosa, Sebastià Junyer-Vidal and Cinto Reventós Sr., as also to all those people who in one way or another have made his work easier.